THE PROFESSIONAL
WRESTLERS'
WORKOUT & INSTRUCTIONAL GUIDE

FOREWORD BY JIM ROSS

HARLEY RACE · RICKY STEAMBOAT · LES THATCHER
WITH ALEX MARVEZ

ELITE PRO WRESTLING TRAINING
Learn from the legends!

SP
SPORTS
PUBLISHING
L.L.C.

www.SportsPublishingLLC.com

ISBN: 1-58261-947-6

Cover photos and instructional photos by Philip Groshong. All other photos courtesy of Les Thatcher and Elite Pro Wrestling Training.

Publishers: Peter L. Bannon and Joseph J. Bannon Sr.
Senior managing editor: Susan M. Moyer
Acquisitions editor: Dean Miller and Dean Reinke
Developmental editor: Elisa Bock Laird
Art director: K. Jeffrey Higgerson
Cover/dust jacket design: Dustin J. Hubbart
Book design: Dustin J. Hubbart
Imaging: Dustin J. Hubbart, Kenneth J. O'Brien
Photo editor: Erin Linden-Levy
Media and promotions managers: Nick Obradovich (regional),
    Randy Fouts (national), Maurey Williamson (print)

Printed in the United States of America

Sports Publishing L.L.C.
804 North Neil Street
Champaign, IL 61820

Phone: 1-877-424-2665
Fax: 217-363-2073
www.SportsPublishingLLC.com

CONTENTS

Many of us who have been in this business longer than a cup of coffee will tell you that this is one of the greatest businesses in the world and for a variety of reasons. Some will espouse the financial rewards of the talented main event level wrestlers I have known who have had *million-dollar months,* which most cannot fathom. Obviously not everyone is going to accomplish those staggering numbers; however, a fundamentally sound and talented wrestler who maintains his motivation, is in great athletic condition, and is always attempting to raise the level of his game can earn a six-figure income in today's marketplace, especially working for a company like World Wrestling Entertainment.

Some wrestlers not only enjoy the financial rewards that this business can provide, but also enjoy traveling to parts of the world that they would not have had the opportunity to do in other lines of work. Our world is an amazing place with many memorable sights, and wrestlers for generations have regarded their worldwide travel as one of the more memorable aspects of this challenging profession.

Another wonderful aspect of this business is the opportunity to build lasting relationships with your peers. I have had the privilege of being in the business for more than 30 years, and I still have friends to this day that I made in year one of my journey in the wrestling business. I have been mentored by a variety of successful people. I learned something different from each of these individuals and have tried to take what I perceived as their best qualities and use them in my own management style within the business. If I was not in this business, I could still use many of the things I have learned to be successful in other walks of life. In general, life's experiences are priceless to begin with, but it seems that this oftentimes wacky and unpredictable business provides more unique life experiences than any profession I have ever been associated with, and I have worked in radio broadcasting, advertising sales, retail sales, and owned a department store.

For all of wrestling's many rewards to come to fruition and be realized, every in-ring performer *must* have fundamentally sound ring skills, in my opinion. Being successful wrestling in a pro ring is a unique art form that takes years to perfect totally. Some folks never get it, while some pick it up as if they were born to be in this business. The point is this: if one is really serious about a successful career in the wrestling business, there has to be an everlasting commitment to the trade to learn the fundamental skills that it takes to get to the promised land. Fundamentals come long before an individual's character development, i.e., their characterization or gimmick. That would be akin to a budding baseball pitcher who develops his mannerisms on the mound before he learns to throw strikes.

This business is not for everyone, and more fail than succeed. You should know that and remember it every day of your career. In sports and in entertainment, individuals are more often than not judged by their last performance. The "What have you done for me lately?" philosophy is and has always been alive and well in the wrestling business; however, wrestling doesn't have the franchise on that matter, for the record.

In order to break into wrestling, one must have the fundamental skills to impress a promoter, and I can assure you that every promoter I have worked for, and there have been some beauts, is *always* looking for new talent with solid fundamental skills with the aptitude to develop a marketable persona to go along with the in-ring skills. I am still a believer that it's what is done bell to bell that really separates the stars from the wannabes. That's the foundation that one's career is built on. Never forget that.

Harley Race, Les Thatcher, and Ricky Steamboat are three men whom I have tremendous respect for. Over my 30-plus years in the business, I have personally been around each of them on a personal and a business level and have worked with each of them at a variety of wrestling companies. Each had his own unique set of skills and personality that separated him from other wrestlers, but the one thing in common for all of these successful and respected wrestling figures is that each of them, in the ring, was exceptionally fundamentally sound. They could adapt their styles to a variety of opponents on any continent, no matter the communication barriers that may have existed and provide the fans and the promoters the desired bang for their buck. I cannot think of three individuals who I would trust more in training dedicated, athletically conditioned men or women than these three legitimate legends of the wrestling business.

There is much more to becoming a long-term, successful wrestler than simply looking good in an eight-by-10 publicity photo. If one is devoid of in-ring skills, trust me when I say that a successful, long-term career in wrestling is not possible. This book can help you get on your journey in which there are no guarantees but limitless potential.

Being a student of the game, maintaining a positive attitude, making intelligent personal choices, being in excellent athletic physical condition, and *having excellent fundamental skills* will provide you the golden opportunity to become part of an awesome industry. For many of you, this is the perfect place to start. Good luck and, hopefully, our paths will cross some day at Wrestlemania!

—Jim Ross
Executive Vice President
World Wrestling Entertainment

First off, wrestling should be on a need-to-know type basis. You will read several things in this book that are outside of the realm of wrestling and have no instructional value. These are things that really shouldn't be discussed.

The photos of the moves are for you to look at and should be used to get an inside look at some of the moves in the industry. Please don't use this book as a sole guide to do these moves. This book should be intriguing to people who are interested in pro wrestling and can be used a foundational knowledge for the business, but make sure you find a credible and capable trainer if you want to move beyond head knowledge and into the ring.

Thank you to Jim Ross for taking the time out of his busy schedule to write the foreword for this book. Thank you to Les Thatcher and Ricky Steamboat, who are two of the more knowledgeable people on the ins and outs of pro wrestling.

—Harley Race

ACKNOWLEDGMENTS

Thirty-one years ago in Minneapolis, Minnesota, I stepped into the basement of a 20-story office building to start my wrestling career. The basement was cold, damp, and in some areas poorly lit. My first thought was, "What am I getting myself into?"—the business surrounded itself with so much mystique and so many unknowns then.

There we stood—16 rookies in all—with the same dream of becoming a superstar in professional wrestling. At the end of two weeks, only four of us remained. Buck Zumhoff, Jan Nelson, Scott Irwin, and me reported to camp each morning to start our five-hour day of training. (Jan Nelson and Scott Irwin have since passed away, but I'm sure they are taking some bumps in a wrestling ring up above.)

Verne Gagne was the promoter and from his camps came great names such as Ken Patera, Jim Brunzell, Greg Gagne, and probably one of the greatest of all time, Ric Flair. My instructor was Khosrow Vaziri, known later as "The Iron Sheik," who also had come from Gagne's camp. Many thanks to "The Iron Sheik" for the time he took to teach me the fundamentals of the business. Throughout my whole career I've had some great matches, but I understand that the guys I worked with were great workers in their own right: Sergeant Slaughter and Don Kernodle, Steve Austin and Brian Pillman, Jack and Jerry Brisco, Paul Jones and Baron Von Raschke, Jimmy Snuka and Ray Stevens, and Arn Anderson and Larry Zbyszko in tags and Bret Hart, Harley Race, Dory Funk, Don Muraco, Mr. Fuji, Randy Savage, Greg Valentine, Steve Keirn, Blackjack Mulligan, Dick Murdock, Dick Slater, Haku, Jake Roberts, and Ric Flair for the countless hours in my single matches. Many thanks to all for allowing me to perform at my highest ability. Thanks also to my two special tag-team partners, Jay Youngblood and Shane Douglas. I must also thank promotion, because without promoters, my name would have not been known on a local and global basis—Jim Crockett with Mid-Atlantic Championship Wrestling, Ted Turner with the World Championship Wrestling, Vince McMahon with the World Wrestling Federation and World Wrestling Entertainment, and Verne Gagne with the American Wrestling Association camp.

Last but not least, I thank Les Thatcher, Harley Race, and Alex Marvez for allowing me to be a part of this book and for bringing the project together.

—Ricky Steamboat

As a young boy who wanted to be a professional wrestler, I never once in my wildest dreams thought I might some day walk into a store and see my name on the dust jacket of a book as an author. For that, I must thank everyone at Sports Publishing L.L.C. for making this a reality.

I have enjoyed this project so much in part because of my co-trainers Harley and "Steamer" who have made working with the future stars of pro wrestling so much fun. Not only are they two of the finest talents ever to grace a ring but great friends and human beings as well.

This book just covers the tip of the iceberg when it comes to learning the art of professional wrestling. But we hope that if you mix it with hundreds of hours of proper instruction in the ring as well as the passion to excel, you will be able to follow your dreams as Harley, Ricky, and I have been able to do.

Thanks to Jim Ross, who humbles the three of us by what he writes in his foreword. Thank God for people like "Good Ol' J.R." who share our love for this crazy business we work in.

Thanks to my newest best friend, Alex Marvez, who brought the same pride to the table in writing for us as we supplied with our in-ring work.

I want to thank Matt Stryker and Nigel McGuinness for serving as our models for conditioning drills and maneuvers. Both are outstanding performers who are two of the brightest young talents in our business. More information on Matt (www.mattstryker.com) and Nigel (www.nigelmcguinness.com) can be found on their websites.

How can I wrap this up without first thanking everyone who touched my career along the 45-year path I traveled to reach this point? I wouldn't trade that time in the grunt and groan business for four years in the best college on this planet. I have been blessed with a job I love to do.

I do want to dedicate this work to my loving father and mother, Sam and Dorothy Malady, who were so supportive of my chasing this dream and most of the time without understanding why. I wish they were here to share this. Lastly, but just as importantly, I dedicate this to my loving wife, Alice, who seems to understand my need to have a lifelong affair with something called professional wrestling. I love you all and hope that those of you who read this can feel the passion that Harley, Ricky, and I left on these pages.

—Les Thatcher

When I was in the second grade, my father, Albert, took me to the Miami Beach Convention Center to catch a card presented by Championship Wrestling from Florida. From that point forward, I was hooked by the grappling game. This book is dedicated to him as well as my mother, Annette, sister, Audrey, and wife, Sherry, for encouraging and tolerating my passion for the industry.

I want to thank Sports Publishing L.L.C., especially our editor Elisa Bock Laird for her diligent work in making this book so sharp and Nick Obradovich for recruiting me for this project. Having the chance to work with Harley, Ricky, and Les was a joy. All three are true professionals and great people I am happy to call my friends. While I have written a pro wrestling column for various newspapers since 1989, I learned more about the inner workings of the business by watching these three veterans work with young trainees than in any other two-day span I had spent around wrestling.

My love of wrestling remains fueled by the *Wrestling Observer Newsletter,* so a special thanks to Dave Meltzer for always providing inspiration both personally and professionally about how to do things the right way. I also wanted to express appreciation to those whom I have gotten to know through the wrestling business, especially Kim Wood, Zane Bresloff, Paul Heyman, Diamond Dallas Page, Howard Brody, Gordon Solie, Mike Rosenthal, Lou and David Sahadi, Bruce Owens, Dr. Mike Brannon, and Norman Smiley, along with the *South Florida Sun-Sentinel* and Scripps-Howard News Service for the strong support they have given my weekly column.

— Alex Marvez

Midway through a training seminar at the Heartland Wrestling Association complex in Evandale, Ohio, Harley Race addressed how he responds when asked whether pro wrestling is real or fake.

"I've always answered that question this way: If you think it's fake, let me take you in that ring and you land like we have to land," he said. "Then, you determine it for yourself."

A storied veteran of more than four decades in the wrestling business, Race then posed his own question.

"You know, I can make you pass out with just two fingers," he said. "Have you ever been in that hold?"

Race proceeds to demonstrate, tucking the volunteer's head in the crook of his shoulder while hooking his two fingers together underneath the chin. Race begins to crank backward, forcing the helpless volunteer to tap out before passing out.

Race then leans back in his folding chair and takes a drag from his cigarette with a smile etched across his weathered face.

Welcome to the real world of professional wrestling, where things aren't always what they seem.

The majority of you reading this book have the same kind of dreams that Race, Ricky Steamboat, and Les Thatcher did years ago: Becoming a wrestling superstar and enjoying all the trappings that go with it.

Fame. Fortune. The chance to tour the United States, possibly even the world. And if you're good enough, having your hand raised in victory in front of thousands of screaming fans with a title belt around your waist.

The knowledge provided in *The Professional Wrestlers' Workout & Instructional Guide* will help you make major strides toward doing so as well.

After reading this book, you should have knowledge of how maneuvers are executed effectively and safely, the physical conditioning needed to perform them, and the thought process involved in piecing together an actual match. You should have an understanding of the psychology of pro wrestling both in and out of the ring and a head start on where to find employment on the independent circuit.

But first things first. Here are some basic tenets you need to understand before proceeding:

• Pro wrestling bouts are not intended as legitimate athletic competition. The match finishes are predetermined. The wrestlers work *together* to ensure the moves are performed properly so neither one gets hurt. Consider wrestling as being just like a well-trained circus act or an athletic soap opera.

• Reading this book alone will *not* make you a pro wrestler. Months of training are required before you are even close to being ready to step into the ring.

• And most importantly: *Holds in this book should not be practiced without the supervision of a qualified trainer. Otherwise, serious injury may occur.*

• All moves should also be executed at a controlled speed. When applying the holds in this book, do so very gently, because all of these moves done improperly can hurt you. Watching a wrestler take another over in a headlock improperly is even more painful to the performers than it is to watch.

MEET THE TRAINERS

Les Thatcher, Harley Race, and Ricky Steamboat

HARLEY RACE

In the storied history of the National Wrestling Alliance, few world champions carry as much respect as Harley Race. He held the title on eight different occasions between 1973 and 1984, including a four-year stretch (1977 to 1981) where he was champion for all but 21 days. Race wrestled his first pro match at age 17 in 1960 following a stint grappling in carnivals that included his involvement in some legitimate matches against local townsfolk who were brave (or foolhardy) enough to try their luck.

Following his memorable stint in the NWA, Race debuted in what was then known as the World Wrestling Federation in 1986. He was billed as "The King" after winning the promotion's second King of the Ring tournament in 1986. Race wrestled with WWF for three more years before the effects of an abdominal injury led to his departure and ultimate retirement. Race later resurfaced in World Championship Wrestling serving in different capacities, including the manager for Leon "Vader" White.

In 1999, Race started his World League Wrestling promotion and opened a training school near his home in Eldon, Missouri. Besides gaining experience to wrestle on the independent circuit, some of Race's best students have landed the chance to work in Japan for the highly respected NOAH promotion.

RICKY "THE DRAGON" STEAMBOAT

One of the top in-ring performers and babyface characters in wrestling history, Ricky Steamboat was a regular headliner wherever he worked from 1977 through his retirement in 1994. Steamboat defeated longtime rival "Nature Boy" Ric Flair to become NWA world champion in 1989, which led to arguably the greatest series of title matches ever held by World Championship Wrestling. Two years earlier, Steamboat had one of the most memorable matches in WWE history when defeating Randy "Macho Man" Savage to win the Intercontinental title at Wrestlemania III. Steamboat was equally adept at tag-team wrestling, as his pairing with the late Jay Youngblood is considered one of the best babyface duos of the late 1970s and early 1980s. Steamboat, whose real name is Richard Blood, became a WWE road agent in late 2004.

LES THATCHER

Les Thatcher wrestled as a top junior heavyweight for more than 20 years (1960 to 1980) in various regional territories. Thatcher held six different regional NWA titles during his career before making the successful transition into other areas of the wrestling business. He worked as a producer, announcer, editor, and author before becoming a trainer in 1993.

Thatcher gained so much prominence in the latter role that he was featured on an MTV wrestling special and hired to run a Cincinnati-based WWE developmental territory (Heartland Wrestling Association) in 2001 and 2002. Thatcher remains a fixture on the independent circuit with his Elite Pro Wrestling Training seminars. His real name is Les Malady.

Thatcher is also the founder of Elite Pro Wrestling Training, which runs clinics/training camps nationwide, using experienced trainers like himself, Harley Race, and Dr. Tom Pritchard of World Wrestling Entertainment fame. More information can be found at www.epwt.com.

BREAKING IN

Here is a basic overview of pro wrestling's evolution and development as a phenomenon, as well as some keys to getting started in the business before you venture into the ring.

The world of pro wrestling is much different than when we began our respective careers. One of the biggest changes is how fans have become wise to the fact that wrestling is a performance art rather than a legitimate sporting competition.

Whether wrestling was fake or real was once a big question mark. Some people didn't think it was real, but others would say, "Nah, this one match between so and so had to be real!" or "In the main event, those guys were really hammering each other!" Wrestlers tried to keep things secret, especially out of the ring.

Previous generations of aspiring wrestlers found it much harder to break into the business because the industry had a closed-shop mentality. Training was often done by the wrestling promoters themselves or their employees, most of whom favored students with amateur wrestling backgrounds.

Regardless of whether they had amateur experience, a student often had to prove his toughness before being allowed to train. It wasn't uncommon for a trainee to suffer minor and even major injuries while being **stretched** by the veterans.

Students usually weren't immediately told that pro wrestling matches were scripted until well into their training. The main reason was the fear that a disgruntled student would expose wrestling secrets to a general public who didn't know how grapplers used the tricks of the trade. Trainees often were told to practice at half speed with the impression given that the actual matches were held at full speed.

Stretching—*n When one performer legitimately dominates another through the use of wrestling or submission holds. Most stretching incidents occur when a wrestler doesn't cooperate with his opponent.*

RING TALK

I broke into the wrestling business in 1974 when a girlfriend became close friends with the daughter of Verne Gagne, an amateur wrestling kingpin who later become the world champion and promoter of his own territory, the Minneapolis-based American Wrestling Association. I was invited to participate in a 10-week training camp being conducted by Khosrow Vaziri, who later became known as the "Iron Sheik."

*We were not told the business was a work until the last day of camp. During camp, they told us to keep **light and loose** when you would grab a*

 (continued)

Light and loose—*adj Indicates when a performer is able to perform crisp-looking holds on his opponent without hurting him.*

headlock or an arm bar. This would allow us to make moves and counters. If I grabbed a headlock and the guy wanted to come around to a top wristlock, he could practice going up and around.

We came to find out on the last day of camp that was the way we actually worked in the ring. I had my suspicions only because Khosrow down the home stretch was dropping subtle hints to us about staying loose and being able to work with your opponent.

—Ricky Steamboat

Few training schools today assume ignorance on the part of the trainees.

Kay fabe—*n The protection of wrestling secrets by its performers. One pro wrestler will tell another to kay fabe when an outsider is in position to hear their conversation.*

RING TALK

I took the mentality of **kay fabe.** I went so far as to not tell my daughter that blood is usually drawn from a self-inflicted wound.

The first time she ever saw her father bleed she was about four years old. I was working in Lexington, Kentucky, for promoter Nick Gulas out of Nashville. She started to scream and cry and holler. My dad had to take her outside and calm her down. After it was over, my dad came to me.

"You've got to tell her what you did," he said.

"No," I said emphatically. "Even if she were an adult, I wouldn't tell her." My mom and dad were stunned.

My daughter is 40 years old, and we still haven't had that conversation. She's smart from reading websites and all that, but I never smartened her up.

—Les Thatcher

"My father went to his grave not being smartened up about this business." —Harley Race

WHAT YOU MAY NOT KNOW

One of the biggest exposés of the wrestling industry came in February 1989. WWE was trying to get its shows reclassified as entertainment rather than sporting events so the promotion wouldn't have to pay taxes to state athletic commissions for sanctioning. The New Jersey Senate received a WWE statement claiming its product was "an activity in which participants struggle hand-in-hand primarily for the purpose of providing entertainment to spectators rather than conducting a bona fide athletic contest."

"Wrestling had been promoted as a sport, but it wasn't true even back when Abraham Lincoln wrestled," WWE owner Vince McMahon said in a 1999 interview with *Cigar Aficionado* magazine. "So I said, 'Let's level with our audience and corporate America.' To *The New York Times,* it was big news. To us, it was a way to tell Madison Avenue, 'This is who we are.'

"Just look at all of the elements on our show. It's action-adventure. But it's also a talk show. Someone else might say it's a cartoon beyond belief. Or it's a soap opera, or a grandiose rock concert. And the athleticism is nothing short of extraordinary. We have no boundaries or limitations. We can go anywhere we want to. We're only limited by our imagination and creativity. We take the best of show biz and roll it all into one."

As pro wrestling became more entertainment oriented, the nature of the product began to change. Different styles such as **hardcore** and the high-flying **lucha libre** from Mexico have become part of today's wrestling scene. Some would even argue that the traditional pro wrestling style is a dying art being replaced by shorter matches with more spectacular moves accompanied by soap-opera storylines with heavy emphasis on sex and violence.

But such a belief is wrong, because wrestling itself remains the backbone behind a successful promotion such as WWE. That means knowing how to perform the basics is a must for anyone who wants to make it in the business.

Think of it like this: A quarterback today still needs the same good foundation as the quarterbacks did decades ago. It's the same for wrestling. Knowing the moves and how to put them in the proper sequence is paramount. Then you can work anyplace.

So many wrestlers today see a neat **bump** and think, "Whee! It's like riding a roller coaster!" Well, that's great. But the best divers in the world learned how to successfully dive off the side of the pool. They didn't jump off a 20-foot tower at first and do a goofy dive. From both a safety factor and just basic learning, they learned how to go into the water the right way. Wrestling is the same way.

That makes selecting the proper trainer so essential. In fact, finding the right teacher may be more difficult than learning how to wrestle.

One of the worst things about the industry nowadays is the high number of unprofessional trainers out there. Some "teachers" buy a ring, rent a warehouse, and say they're trainers even though they've never received adequate training themselves. There is seemingly a promotion or school on every street corner.

Because wrestling is a performance art that generally falls outside of jurisdiction from state athletic commissions, there sometimes isn't an easy way to find a quality training school, let alone check the credentials of the trainers themselves. Here is what you should look for when selecting an instructor:

- Ask around: In a business based upon deceiving fans into believing wrestling is real, it shouldn't be surprising that some trainers aren't honest about where they have wrestled or who the students are that they have taught. You have to find out if the potential trainer knows more about the industry than you do.

SELECTING A TRAINER

Hardcore—*n A bloody style of wrestling that includes the heavy use of weapons and props like barbed wire, chairs, thumbtacks, and even staple guns. Hardcore wrestling is highly discouraged for aspiring wrestlers because of the injury risk.*

Lucha libre—*n A style of wrestling popularized in Mexico. Lucha libre wrestling is heavy in flying maneuvers with touches of brawling and submission holds.*

Bump—*n The fall that a performer takes.*

TIP

Some training schools that charge a fee for an introductory workout may try to take your money by roughhousing and hoping you don't return.

• A trainer should have a legitimate background. Don't let someone tell you, "Oh, you wouldn't know me. I wrestled under a mask as Dr. X." If you can't get recommendations from somebody who already is noteworthy in the business, steer clear of that trainer. That eliminates a lot of people.

• You should look for a trainer who is on your side rather than one using you for what essentially amounts to a workout dummy. There are trainers who will say, "Let me show you this bump," and continue to have you take the submissive role while all he is doing is helping himself train. The emphasis is on him, rather than you, and results in a lack of learning for you.

• Training takes time. A pro wrestler isn't born overnight.

There are many aspects that go into becoming a good professional wrestler, and it will take time to develop the physical and mental skills needed to sell a match. In fact, it should take months of training before you are ready to make your debut. So if a trainer tells you that you can become a wrestler in one month, stay away!

• Safety: Sadly, there are occasional stories of a student death during pro wrestling training. Selecting the wrong trainer also can increase the chance you may get injured. There are some 21-year-old students who are gimping around with ailments that may never heal.

Training should begin with easy drills and should be limited to mat work to minimize the risk of injury. If a trainer tries to have you jump off the top rope doing 450-degree splashes without even showing you what a headlock is, find a new trainer!

The same goes for any trainer who pitches chair shot practice or any other drills that could cause you bodily harm. Hitting an opponent with a chair in a way that won't cause physical damage is a technique that should be learned much later in training.

WHAT YOU MAY NOT KNOW

The importance of safe training was reemphasized in July 2005 when a California jury awarded the family of Brian Ong a $1.34 million settlement in a wrongful death lawsuit against the Pacific Coast Sports wrestling school after the 27-year-old was killed during a training session.

The five-foot-eight, 175-pound Ong died in 2001 after landing incorrectly when taking a bump from the seven-foot, 400-pound Dalip "Giant" Singh, who would later play the role of Turley in the 2005 remake of *The Longest Yard*. Ong had been training for only nine weeks when he was killed.

A press release from the law firm that represented Ong stated he was fatally injured "as a result of being thrown to the mat twice after being asked to volunteer to 'receive' a professional wrestling move (called the 'flapjack') ... The evidence showed that Brian Ong 'had his bell rung,' meaning having some sort of head injury and being woozy and disoriented after being thrown to the mat the first time he tried the move and was killed after being thrown the second time."

The *Wrestling Observer Newsletter* reported that two other students were injured trying to take the same bump from Singh, whose pro wrestling training was being fast-tracked because of his potential marketability and size.

"This class was more to teach Singh and use the students as dummies than an instructional class," *Observer* writer/publisher Dave Meltzer wrote.

Pacific Coast Sports, which is connected with the All Pro Wrestling promotion in California, is a well-known training center that is still considered a quality school. But Ong's death should serve as proof of what can happen when even experienced trainers make a mistake in judgment. Students also should know their limitations.

When wrestling promotions offer a disclaimer not to try moves at home without proper supervision, it is not just an idle comment to make the industry seem more dangerous. It is a very truthful fact.

- Personality: Just like in sports, athletes react in different ways to the personalities of their coaches. Because pro wrestling requires such hands-on training, it's important to have a solid level of trust and respect with the person who is teaching you. If you cannot connect with your trainer, try finding someone else who is a better fit.

- Cost: There is no set cost when it comes to how much you should pay for wrestling training. But by and large, the expression, "You pay for what you get," applies to wrestling schools.

  Be wary of the trainer who tries to charge you a large fee for an introductory workout. For six months of training, expect to pay in the range of $3,000 to $4,000 if working with a reputable teacher. If you are not ready by that time, your trainer should be willing to allow you to continue training for a nominal fee until you're ready to step inside the ring. But if you're lax in your training and don't attend classes on a consistent basis, don't be surprised if the trainer tries to cut ties with you—sometimes before you've even wrestled in front of a live audience.

WHAT YOU MAY NOT KNOW

Al Snow's teaching prowess toward aspiring wrestlers was showcased during WWE's *Tough Enough* series. But when he joined WWE on a full-time basis in 1998, Snow (Allen Sarven) cut ties with the Lima, Ohio, training school he ran before making it to the big time.

"Basically, the first lesson I was taught [as a trainer] is to separate the mark and his money as quickly as possible," Snow said in a 2001 interview with Scripps-Howard News Service. "But I think it would be kind of wrong to represent to people that 'Hey, it's my school,' when they're not going to be trained by me when I'm not going to be there.

"It has taken me a long time to build a reputation in the business. Whenever you train somebody, the way I was taught, they now carry a little piece of your reputation with them. I don't want anybody to say Al Snow trained them when I didn't really train them. The money would be awfully nice, but it all could come back to bite you in the rear end."

Here are some of the top independent promotions and training schools where aspiring talent can hone its skills and potentially land a spot on cards these groups run.

Booker T and Stevie Ray's Pro Wrestling Academy
2301 Commerce
Houston, TX 77251
Telephone: 713-222-0588
Website: www.btsrwrestlingacademy.com

Border City Wrestling/Can-Am Wrestling School
760 Roseland Drive South
Windsor, Ontario, Canada N9G 1T8
Telephone: (519) 969-1245
Website: www.bordercitywrestling.com

Chaotic Wrestling and Chaotic Training Center
100 Belmont Street
North Andover, MA 01845
Telephone: 978-685-7173
Website: www.chaoticwrestling.com

Coastal Championship Wrestling
2362 N.W. 120th Lane
Coral Springs, FL 33065
Telephone: 954-275-1334
Website: www.coastalchampionshipwrestling.com

East Coast Wrestling Association
2612 Christiana Meadows
Bear, DE 19701
Telephone: 302-325-1592
Website: www.ecwaprowrestling.com

Four-Star Championship Wrestling
5071 S State Road 7, Bay 711
Davie, FL 33314
Telephone: 954-288-2098 or 954-579-8696
Website: www.fscw.net

The Funking Conservatory
2200 N.E. 36 Avenue
Ocala, FL 34470
Telephone: 352-895-4658
Website: www.dory-funk.com

Fusion Pro Wrestling/Altitude Pro Wrestling Training
1271 S. Uravan Street
Aurora, CO 80017
Telephone: 303-981-3563 or 303-667-6822
Website: www.fusionprowrestling.com

Heartland Wrestling Association
10800 Reading Rd., Suite A
Cincinnati, OH 45241
Telephone: 513-771-1650
Website: www.hwaonline.com

The Ron Hutchison Professional Wrestling Academy at Sully's Gym
300 Coxwell Ave.
Toronto, Ontario, Canada M4L 2A0
Telephone: 416-534-8723
Website: www.angelfire.com/biz/wrestlingschool

Memphis Wrestling
C/O UPN 30 WLMT
2701 Union Ave. Ext.
Memphis, TN 38112
Telephone: 901-795-0722
Website: www.kinglawler.com

Pro Wrestling Iron
895 B Street, No. 431
Hayward, CA 94541
Telephone: 510-670-0504
Website: www.prowrestlingiron.com

PWF Mayhem/Squared Circle Academy
2051 Smith Street
North Providence, RI 02911
Telephone: 401-474-2895
Website: www.pwfnortheast.com

Ring of Honor Wrestling
P.O. Box 1127
Bristol, PA 19007
Telephone: 215-781-2500
Website: www.rohwrestling.com

Slamtech Wrestling University
C/O Bob Evans
1299 G.A.R. Highway
Swansea, MA 02777
Telephone: 508-335-6634
Website: www.slamtechwrestling.com

Stampede Wrestling
Suite 727
105, 150 Crowfoot Crescent NW
Calgary, Alberta, Canada T3G 3T2
Telephone: 403-247-6274
Website: www.stampedewrestling.com

Steve Keirn's Pro Wrestling School of Hard Knocks
945 Alexander Ave.
Port Orange, FL 32129
Telephone: 386-383-0265
Website: www.prowrestlingschoolofhardknocks.com

Storm Wrestling Academy
PO Box 58013
Chaparral RPO
Calgary, Alberta, Canada T2X 3V2
Website: www.stormwrestling.com

Texas Wrestling Academy
P.O. Box 760542
San Antonio, TX 78245
Telephone: 210-273-4110
Website: www.geocities.com/etwmaster/index.html

Ultimate Pro Wrestling
113 S. Sierra
El Segundo, CA 90245
Telephone: 949-475-7663; 310-322-5552
Website: www.upw.com

The Wild Samoan Training Center
P.O. Box 251
Whitehall, PA 18052 -0251
Telephone: 610-435-1666
Website: www.wildsamoan.com

World League Wrestling
119 South Maple
Eldon, MO 65026
Telephone: 573-392-4100
Website: www.harleyrace.com

STRENGTH AND CONDITIONING

Figuratively, most aspiring wrestlers want to run before they can walk. Being in good physical condition before beginning training will make learning much easier. It reduces the risk of injury and allows for more in-ring work during a session. Some beginners can't even work a 10-minute match. They have to start slow because they're sucking wind. Don't let that happen to you.

The following chapter will provide an outline on how to get into better shape and maintain that conditioning as well as warmup drills and stretching exercises that will help prevent injuries. We also will look at the importance of a good physique and what role anabolic steroids play in the industry.

WRESTLING WARMUPS

It is all about stretching. No, we're not talking about the wrestling term. But having a sound pre-match routine gives you a fighting chance to succeed in the wrestling business.

When wrestlers were working six to seven nights a week in the day of regional promotions, extensive stretching wasn't as important, because most performers already were limber from having matches on a consistent basis. The same goes for cardiovascular training in a gym, because most wrestlers stayed fit by working 20-minute bouts on a nightly basis.

Because few of today's wrestlers work that kind of schedule, it's essential to stretch. Muscle pulls can often be traced to wrestlers not being limber enough before stepping into the ring. After a 10-minute warmup session, like riding a stationary bike or a light jog, extensive stretching is recommended to help reduce the risk of injury. A good stretching session should take about 20 to 25 minutes to complete.

Areas of special emphasis should include the hamstrings and groin, because those can be especially vulnerable to pulls without proper stretching. There are several stretches you can do to warm up the legs and groin:

• Toe touches

Description: Toe touches are used to stretch the hamstrings. While standing with your feet close together (**1**), slowly reach down and touch your toes (**2**). Hold the stretch for 20 to 25 seconds and release.

If that exercise is difficult or causes back pain, lie on your back with both knees bent. Lift one foot toward the ceiling while keeping your knee slightly bent. Clasp your hands behind the knee for support. You should feel the hamstring stretching in the back of your thigh. Repeat with the other leg.

• Leg swings

Description: Stand with your right hand touching a wall for balance. Swing your left leg forward and backward 10 to 12 times. When completed, place your left hand against the wall and swing your right leg forward and backward 10 to 12 times.

• Quadriceps pulls

Description: Stand on your left leg. Lift your right leg and place your right hand on your right ankle (**1**). Pull your right leg so that the heel of your right foot is touching the back of your right thigh (**2**). Hold for 20 seconds and then stretch your left leg in similar fashion.

• Butterfly Stretches
 Description: Butterfly stretches are suggested to warm up the groin. Sit on the ground with your heels touching each other. Place light pressure on your knees, pushing them toward the ground **(1).** This will stretch the groin and hip flexors.

Recommended stretching exercises for the upper body focus primarily on the arms, back, and neck. The lower back can be stretched by sitting cross-legged on the floor and slowly leaning forward so your arms are reaching over your legs. The objective is to be able to place your forearms on the floor in front of you and keep them there for the stretch. Stretching your neck can be done from a sitting position with your knees touching the ground. Move your chin toward your chest and keep it close for 10 seconds. Slowly move your head back to its regular position. Tilt your head to the left in a fashion that will place your left ear on top of your left shoulder. Repeat to the right. Complete the exercise by rotating your neck clockwise in a slow fashion. To stretch your arms, clasp your hands together behind your back and try lifting them up toward your head. Hold for 10 seconds and then release.

Hip flexors also shouldn't be ignored. Exercises should be chosen that improve flexibility without causing extreme discomfort or injury.

WHAT YOU MAY NOT KNOW

One of the most flexible performers in the wrestling business is Rob Van Dam, who has starred in WWE since 2001. A fan of martial arts films as a teenager, Van Dam (real name Rob Stazkowsky) began stretching to try to emulate the moves he was seeing on the screen.

After initially struggling to complete a split, Van Dam placed his legs on two chairs in his mother's kitchen and balanced himself by holding a broomstick. Not only could he eventually complete a split, Stazkoswky later set a world record for what became known as the Van Dam Lift.

With his legs split on two chairs, Van Dam had to bend over to pick a dumbbell off the ground, then straighten his back to bring himself up, and lift the weight to his stomach. In 1998, Van Dam performed a lift of 166.5 pounds that set a record for the International All-Around Weightlifting Association.

Van Dam said he spends roughly 40 to 45 minutes a day stretching and tries to remain flexible through some unusual routines such as bending over and picking up his foot or using his foot to flush a toilet rather than his hand.

"Over the years, I've had all kinds of guys come up to me and tell me how they would like to stretch out more, but they never do," Van Dam said on the website to his comic book store (www.5starcomics.com)."I always figured that's why I don't get hurt as much [as other wrestlers] when I'm in the ring.

"I put myself through a pretty rigorous routine from early on, and it involves a lot. I roll back on my neck, do the split, lift my feet up off the ground, and tie myself in knots. It's all part of my daily routine, so by the time I get to the ring, I'm ready for anything."

Just like other athletes before playing their respective sports, stretching and warming up properly are a must for professional wrestlers. Before you enter the ring, you need to make sure that you follow a specific protocol to get your body ready to perform the maneuvers in the ring.

The following routine will help you get prepared to enter the ring by ensuring that all of the muscles you use in ring work will be limber:

• 40 jumping jacks

Description: This exercise is designed to raise your heart rate, so don't take shortcuts. Make every jack count with crisp movements with your arms and legs **(1, 2)**.

• 50 Hindu squats

Description: This exercise and the squats mentioned below will play a major role in building your conditioning as well as strengthening your legs. To perform Hindu squats properly, from a standing position (**1**), drop into a deep squat with your hands behind you while standing on the balls of your feet (**2**). As you rise, brings your hands forward while coming to stand on your heels (**3**). Repeat without resting and gradually build sets and repetitions.

WHAT YOU MAY NOT KNOW

Hindu squats have been used by some wrestling trainers to weed out students who were not able to master a requested amount—as many as 500—in one continuous stretch. The late Hiro Matsuda, who trained stars such as Hulk Hogan, Lex Luger, and Ron "Faarooq" Simmons, was a stickler for physical conditioning. Matsuda was a top talent in Japan and the United States, particularly in Florida, while wrestling for more than 20 years and serving as a minority owner in the Championship Wrestling from Florida promotion. Matsuda, whose real name was Yasuhiro Kojima, made Hindu squats one of the most important exercises for himself and the students he trained.

• 30 push-ups

There are several versions of this standard exercise. Push-ups can be done with the feet or upper body elevated **(1, 2).** Elbows also can be positioned both wider and closer than normal. All of these variations provide different ways to develop the muscles worked in standard push-ups.

TIP

Don't cheat. Bring your body all of the way down and maintain proper form while avoiding bad habits, like arching your back.

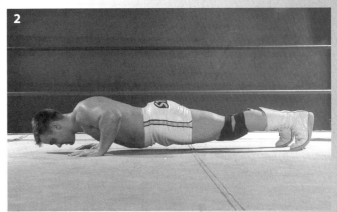

WHAT YOU MAY NOT KNOW

Ex-Cincinnati Bengal strength coach Kim Wood, who helped the late "Flyin'" Brian Pillman break into the wrestling business during the mid-1980s, said he is sometimes asked to design workout programs by those trying to get into better shape. Wood tells them to perform 50 push-ups, 50 Hindu squats, and 50 sit-ups each day for a year. Wood said the 50-50-50 workout will result in a noticeable physical improvement if performed over an extended period of time. This regimen can be especially helpful to the novice wrestler who is trying to work into better shape before beginning serious training.

• 50 quarter-squats

Description: These are not as grueling as Hindu squats, although it may feel that way after performing those repetitions earlier in the warmups. From a standing position (**1**) drop only one quarter of the way down on these squats (**2**). The key to this exercise is making sure you bend your knees while standing erect, so that the squat works the thighs and gluteus maximus.

• 20 mountain climbers

Description: While in a push-up position, shuffle your legs so it looks like you are climbing a mountain (**1, 2**). Like with the jumping jacks, this helps accelerate the heart rate and improves the warmup before in-ring training begins.

• 25 half-squats

Description: Start each repetition in a standing position (**1**) and then drop down to a half-squat position (**2**) to finish the exercise.

• 10 bend-and-thrusts

Description: This is arguably the most grueling of the warmup exercises. Do a deep squat, lunge into position for a push-up, and bounce back to your feet.

• 10 leg lifts

Description: Lie flat on your back with your hands underneath the tailbone (**1**), then lift your legs off the ground to work the abdominal muscles (**2**). The legs should be kept together and not spread apart.

• 100 sit-ups/stomach crunches

Description: The first 50 work the major abdominal muscles, while the other 50 should be done to emphasize other portions of the abdomen. Lie flat on the floor with your hands clasped behind your head. Keep your feet/knees in the air to help alleviate the pressure this exercise places on your lower back (**1**). Move your head forward as though you were trying to touch your chin to the base of your neck (**2**). Return to your original position and repeat for the first 50 repetitions. For the next 50 repetitions, alternate twisting to try to bring your right elbow to touch your left knee (**3**) and your left elbow to your right knee (**4**).

WHAT YOU MAY NOT KNOW

When it comes to abdominal workouts among pro wrestlers, one of the most legendary was done by Angelo Poffo. The father of grapplers Randy "Macho Man" Savage and "The Genius" Lanny Poffo, Angelo Poffo performed sit-ups continually for four hours and 10 minutes during one workout in 1945. Poffo finished with 6,033 sit-ups, earning him honors from the U.S. Navy and an appearance in a "Ripley's Believe it or Not" cartoon.

• 5 x 5 x 5

Description: This is a good in-ring warmup drill for students who have advanced beyond the basics of their training.

The first "5": Wrestler A should take Wrestler B from rope to rope five consecutive times without releasing him (**1**). A kick to the abdomen can be used as a transition move when trading off on sending a wrestler into the ropes. Run this drill at a controlled speed fast enough to gain some cardiovascular benefits without compromising on form and body language.

The second "5": Wrestler A whips Wrestler B into the ropes (**2**). Wrestler A then drops to his stomach (slapping the mat with his hand in the process to generate noise) so Wrestler B can jump over him (**3**). Wrestler A gets up and executes a leapfrog when Wrestler B bounces back off the ropes (**4**). Wrestler A should be sure to spread his legs wide enough to allow Wrestler B, who should be carefully ducking, sufficient room to pass underneath without making contact to the groin area. Repeat four more times.

The third "5": These are also known as *up-and-overs*. Wrestler A should grab Wrestler B and whip him toward the turnbuckle. Wrestler B should stop before reaching the corner, grab the ropes on each side of **turnbuckle,** and lift himself in the air by either leaping or bouncing off the bottom rope if more spring is necessary (**5**). Wrestler A should then run underneath Wrestler B into the corner, stopping before hitting the turnbuckle. Repeat four more times.

Turnbuckle—*n A turnbuckle is metal of varying sizes with hooks on each end and is threaded in the middle. Covered with padding, it is used to tighten the ring ropes and hold them. There are three buckles to each corner. They connect to the ring post through an eyebolt and an O-ring on the rope.*

TIP

Always wipe your feet while standing on the edge of the ring apron before entering.

CARDIOVASCULAR TRAINING

One of the most embarrassing things that can happen to a wrestler is the inability to finish a match because of a lack of conditioning. You can look like Arnold Schwarzenegger did in his heyday, but if you've got a six-minute match and in three or four minutes you're out of gas and can't carry on, the match could finish in a way you do not want it to.

Some cardiovascular work will be done in the ring. Jogging, riding a bicycle, using an elliptical machine, or running stairs away from wrestling are exercises that will increase your endurance. Try any of those exercises to a point where you are comfortable and not short of breath and/or dizzy. Ideally, you will be able to perform each exercise for at least 20 minutes three to five times a week. Cardiovascular routines need to be upped once in a while to increase your endurance and so you do not plateau. Jogging, sprinting, running stairs, and Hindu squats are all exercises to build conditioning that can be done outside a gym. Sets of wind sprints of 40 to 60 yards will help make sure you are conditioned for the short-term burst needed at times during a match, like when a **babyface** is making a comeback. If you are on a road trip, run the stairs of the hotel for cardio-vascular training.

Still, there is no substitute for **ring wind.** That is where you need a combination of stamina and short-energy bursts as well as experience controlling the adrenaline that comes with working in front of an audience.

TIP

Stretching is especially important before sprinting to avoid pulling muscles.

Babyface—*n A good-guy wrestler whose character is intended to be cheered on by the crowd.*

Ring wind—*n The conditioning that is built by actually wrestling in a match or stepping inside the ring.*

WEIGHT TRAINING

Even if aided by anabolic steroids, top-flight wrestlers don't obtain their chiseled physiques simply by digesting supplements or illegal muscle-enhancing substances. You might not have the body type or genetics for a million-dollar physique, but that isn't an excuse for not trying to look in shape. Extensive gym work is required, with some of today's wrestlers dedicating one day a week toward just one particular body part like a competitive bodybuilder would.

Consult with your doctor before beginning a training/weight-lifting program. If you need to gain weight, lean muscle mass looks much better than just bulk weight. Lean muscle mass also makes you look larger without carrying fat weight and retaining water. If you are carrying too much body fat and want to become leaner, you will want to replace the fat you lose with lean muscle.

If you train properly, working a body part or muscle group (chest, back, biceps, etc.) once a week can be enough. Here are some keys to follow:

• Training intensity must be good. Train hard and heavy enough with good form to exhaust the muscle group. Always use proper form in all movements. Sloppy form just to move more weight can get you hurt.

- Consume proper nutrition to help your body recover and muscles grow in size as well as become stronger.

- Perform a warmup set before each exercise that includes multiple repetitions with a lighter weight. Make sure those repetitions also are done with the proper form.

- Rest between sets should be between 45 seconds and one minute, except on your heaviest sets where you do no more than one or two reps. In that situation, you can take as much as two minutes of rest.

- Do some form of aerobic exercise at least three times per week, like biking, jogging, walking, etc. This helps burn fat, keeps your heart in shape, and improves your wind when doing wrestling training.

- Your training session should last no longer than 45 minutes to one hour when training one body part at a time.

If you have never weight trained before, do not try to start with the enclosed sample workout. Ask your wrestling trainer for an entry-level program to get you started and then build to a harder regimen.

Adjustments should be made in the sample training schedule depending on your body type, needs, job, and type of equipment you have to train on. An average week should look like this:

Monday: Legs
Tuesday: Chest and front deltoids, abdomen, half-hour of aerobic training
Wednesday: Back and rear deltoids
Thursday: Biceps, half-hour of aerobic training
Friday: Triceps, abdomen
Saturday or Sunday: Half-hour or hour of aerobic training

You might not have that kind of time to invest in weight training, especially if you have a full-time job. But that doesn't mean you can't look muscular with a shorter training schedule. Home exercise can be done with an adjustable workout bench and a set of dumbbells. PowerBlocks are recommended because they are adjustable, allowing you to use different weight increments for different exercises. There also are different types of workout bands and rubber cables that are portable and provide solid resistance for a variety of exercises. However, if you do not have a home gym, it's recommended that you acquire gym membership and work out there. Working out every other day is sufficient. This will give your body time to recover and effectively build muscle. In the gym, the exercises you do for a body part stretch and tear down muscle tissue. As you rest that body part and give it proper nutrition, it will increase in strength and/or size over a period of time. If you train a body part every day or more then twice per week (once per week is plenty if the workload and intensity level is high), chances are you are overtraining, which has no benefit.

You should be able to train two body parts in an hour to 1:15 at the gym if you're training seriously. If you're training a body part properly, once a week is enough. Basic exercises that should be incorporated into weight-room workouts include biceps curls, bench presses, pull-downs, and triceps extensions:

• Biceps curls

Description: When performing a biceps curl, make sure your arm is stretched out (**1**). Bring the weight toward your shoulder, bending your elbow in the process (**2a, 2b**).

• Bench presses

Description: The bench press is done with a bar that is suspended on a bench. With your back on the bench, lift the weight **(1),** and bring it to your chest **(2)**. Lift the weight so your arms are extended and repeat.

• Pull-downs

Description: From a sitting position and with your hands gripping the outside of the bar in a spot that is comfortable for you **(1)**, pull the bar down toward your chest **(2)** and let it rise back toward a resting position. Repeat. This exercise helps develop your back muscles. Several different upper-body muscles can be worked through other exercises on a pull-down machine.

• Triceps extensions

Description: To work your left triceps from a standing position, lift your left arm into the air while holding a dumbbell that you can handle **(1)**. For support, place your right hand on your left biceps while positioning your right forearm across your forehead **(2)**. Lower the weight to your left shoulder blade **(3)**, raise it back above your head, and repeat. Reverse the arm positioning to work the right triceps. Make sure your posture is erect while performing this exercise.

Leg exercises such as curls and extensions are recommended for building and toning the lower body.

• Leg curls
Description: A leg curl is designed to work the hamstring. Lying on your stomach, slowly curl your heels toward your buttocks while your legs are behind roller pads on an exercise machine.

• Leg extensions
Description: A leg extension is designed to work the quadriceps. Place your lower shins behind a roller on a workout machine. Extend your leg forward to a point just before your legs are completely straight. Return to the starting position and repeat.

TIP

Temper these exercises if you are doing heavy in-ring training. Otherwise, you may be dead-legged in the ring.

TIP

The wrestler who gets booked for a road trip that requires an overnight stay can bring dumbbells in his car for an in-room workout.

Here is a sample advance workout. A beginner should not immediately try this but build up to it. Also, don't stick to a set routine forever. Change the routine around every few months so as to not allow the muscle group to become accustomed to any one routine, because it will stagnate your development.

Monday—Legs
Leg press or squats: five sets of 20, 6, 6, 10, 15 repetitions
Leg extensions: four sets of 15, 12, 8, 6 repetitions
Leg curls: four sets of 15, 12, 8, 6 repetitions
Calf raises: five sets of 30, 20, 10, 6, 6 repetitions

Tuesday—Chest and front deltoids, and abdomen
Incline machine or barbell press: five sets of 20, 6, 6, 10, 15 repetitions
Flat-bench dumbbell press: four sets of 15, 12, 8, 6 repetitions
Dips between bars (elbows out): four sets to failure
Seated dumbbell press: four sets of 12, 10, 8, 6 repetitions
Front dumbbell raise: four sets of 12, 12, 12, 12 repetitions
Lying six-inch leg raises: three sets of 20, 20, 20 repetitions
Abdominal crunches: three sets of 20, 20, 20 repetitions

Wednesday—Back and rear deltoids
Wide-grip chin-ups: four sets to failure
Bent-over barbell rows (reverse grip): four sets of 15, 12, 6, 6 repetitions
Seated low row: four sets of 15, 6, 6, 15 repetitions
Kneeling one-arm dumbbell rows: four sets of 10, 10, 10, 10 repetitions
Upright barbell rows: four sets of 12, 10, 8, 6 repetitions
Bent-over dumbbell laterals: four sets of 12, 12, 12, 12 repetitions

Thursday—Biceps
Straight bar drag curls: five sets of 20, 6, 6, 10, 15 repetitions
Incline dumbbell curls (both arms): three sets of 15, 10, 6 repetitions
Dumbbell hammer curls: four sets of 10, 10, 10, 10 repetitions

Friday—Triceps and abdomen
Close-grip bench press: four sets of 20, 6, 6, 15 repetitions
One-arm French curls: four sets of 15, 10, 8, 6 repetitions
Dumbbell kickbacks: four sets of 10, 10, 10, 10 repetitions
Lying six-inch leg raises: three sets of 20, 20, 20 repetitions
Abdominal crunches: three sets of 20, 20, 20 repetitions

A GOOD PHYSIQUE

Another benefit of a good training program is that it provides wrestlers with the proper body style for pro wrestling. Today looking toned and strong is just as important as being able to execute the moves. As a beginner in pro wrestling, you must be committed to taking the steps necessary to project the healthy, powerful aura of an esteemed grappler.

One of the ways is to institute a weight-training program like the one mentioned above and to combine it with the adherence to a strict diet.

NUTRITION

Maintaining a strict food regimen is a must; otherwise, much of the time spent in the gym is meaningless when it comes to enhancing physical appearance. Not only will it ensure that you are the best-looking that you can be, it will provide you with the maximum amount of energy needed to perform in the ring.

If you are seeking to lose weight and/or change your diet, here are some simple guidelines that will help you stay in better-than-average shape with below-average body fat. However, it's recommended you speak with your doctor about what kind of diet is right for you.

- Eat five to six small meals daily at intervals of every three to three and a half hours.

- Each meal should have a low-fat protein, starchy carbohydrate, and fibrous carbohydrate. A recommended whole foods list is on the next page.

- Plan meals so that those with the highest amount of starchy carbohydrates are eaten before your highest activity times, like workouts or wrestling training. Keep the starchy carbohydrates lower or out of the meals before your lowest activity time, like your last meal before bed, etc.

- To gain or maintain muscle, you should get at least one gram of protein per pound of body weight per day. So if you weigh 200 pounds, you should consume 200 grams of protein as a starting point. As time goes on, you may have to increase your protein intake to gain lean mass.

- To lose fat, cut back on starchy carbohydrate calories over the entire day and increase your aerobic activity, like running, biking, etc.

- An average meal should have low fat, medium carbohydrates, and medium high protein.

- Read labels on all food products so you can keep your fat intake low. Some foods are higher in fat than you would believe.

- Drink plenty of water each day to flush your system.

Here are three categories of whole foods when planning your meals. Pick at least one food from each category for each meal on your menu. Fruits are not listed, because fructose (fruit sugar) is a simple carbohydrate and in large amounts may be converted to fat in the body quite easily. Enjoy your fruit, but if you are cutting body fat, you may want to limit your intake and at some point eliminate it altogether for a period of time.

- Low-fat proteins: Chicken breast, turkey breast, egg whites, haddock, halibut, cod, crab, lobster, red snapper, scallops, shrimp, swordfish, tuna, round steak (95-percent lean), buffalo, very low-fat sugar-free protein powder (whey meal planning, egg, or egg and milk).

- Starchy carbohydrates: White potatoes, sweet potatoes, corn, oatmeal (rolled oats), lima beans, red beans, black-eyed peas, whole-wheat flour, lentils, peas, popcorn, brown rice, white rice, acorn squash, butternut squash, tomatoes, shredded wheat, yams.

- Fibrous carbohydrates: Green beans, broccoli, carrots, cauliflower, cabbage, celery, lettuce, mushrooms, spinach, chard, summer squash, zucchini, green and red peppers.

Here is a sample menu.

Meal One
Two ounces of oatmeal or oat bran, six egg whites scrambled, two slices of whole-wheat toast with no spreads or toppings, banana or strawberries, coffee or tea.

Meal Two
Chicken breast (boneless, skinless), baked potato or yam, carrots, iced tea.

Meal Three
Ground turkey, pasta, green beans, diet soda.

Meal Four
Chicken breast, protein shake, peas, spinach, iced tea.

Meal Five
White fish, large tossed salad, coffee.

Evening snack
Two or three flavored rice cakes or air-popped popcorn.

RING TALK

I was a competitive bodybuilder in the late 1970s and early 1980s when I was also wrestling professionally. Amazingly, I was able to perform at a high level in both despite a bodybuilding diet that demanded I consume minimal amounts of carbohydrates each day.

To help alleviate being weak in the course of a match, I would eat two or three pieces of fruit beforehand. They were simple carbohydrates that gave me a little sugar rush and would not bloat me. When I was wrestling 20 to 30 minutes, there were times guys would carry me and put me in a bear hug because I was going to pass out. I would ask them to give me a moment because I was so weak. Fruit helped me out. Fruit also is good to eat even when you're going to work out at a gym. You'd like to put something in your system before you go besides a hamburger.

—Ricky Steamboat

For more information about diet and nutrition contact Parillo Performance at 513-874-3305 or www.parillo.com

MUSCLE-ENHANCING DRUGS

Just as the style of today's pro wrestling matches has changed, so have the expectations when it comes to physical appearance.

Anabolic steroids and other muscle-building substances have become as common to the wrestling business as headlocks and pinfalls. Although the industry had its share of users in the 1960s and 1970s, with "Superstar" Billy Graham admittedly among the most notable, steroids boomed in the 1980s with the proliferation of muscle-laden talent taking the spots of performers who learned that big bodies often overshadowed in-ring talent.

Fans began believing that more muscles meant more toughness, even though that often wasn't the case. Those expectations have raised pressure on some performers to begin taking anabolic steroids.

"This was about the time in the mid- to late 1980s that they were going with super-heavyweights like Hulk Hogan and Andre the Giant [as main-event talent]. The matches I used to have in the NWA took me an hour to develop. You could shorten it up, but WWE was getting away from the wrestling part and wanting more of the entertainment part.

"I went on a six-week cycle of steroids. At the end of that six weeks, I said, 'Who cares what I look like? This is not for me. My joints are hurting.' I got away from it."
—Harley Race

Steroids are defined as a group of synthetic hormones that are usually injected or taken orally. They promote the storage of protein and the growth of tissue. Use of steroids leads to increased muscle size and strength among athletes, but also carries a slew of health risks such as sterility and liver damage. Athletes who take steroids also may be more susceptible to torn muscles.

Is it hard work to get muscular and lean without drugs? Yes. But how bad do you want it? Steroids also may put more stress on your joints and tendons, which the drugs don't make larger. Plus, if you don't eat or train right, you can take all of the drugs in the world and not look like a physical specimen.

And most importantly, you still have to have talent in the ring. It's like a baseball player with bulging arms. He's still got to have the ability to hit a curveball to make it.

RING TALK

I admit to having used steroids during my career. My use stems from my days in competitive bodybuilding during the late 1970s. I stopped taking steroids by the late 1980s.

I know some guys obviously take them. You can just tell by the way they look. But I don't think you need to take them. There are more guys in the business not taking them than those who are.

There are guys who take steroids and can't work a lick. All of the needles you stick in you or pills you take are not going to help you. You may walk out to the ring looking great, but as soon as the bell sounds, if you can't work, the fans won't care.

In wrestling, I felt I did not need them. I did for competitive bodybuilding. I had always relied on my work in wrestling to keep me at a main-event level. I was only five foot 11 and weighed 225 pounds. But I knew through my work in the course of a match, I could grow to be six foot five and 280 and project myself that way."

—Ricky Steamboat

MANEUVERS

Even the greatest performers in wrestling had to start somewhere. Now that warmups and stretching are completed, you are ready to begin training by learning how to hit the ropes, fall safely, and execute maneuvers. We will begin with the basics and then gradually move to more complicated wrestling moves. The final section covers cheats.

ROPE WORK

Ring ropes are generally made of steel cables covered with rubber. But the ropes in WWE are slightly different. WWE rings use real rope made of fiber and wrapped with gaffers tape.

These ropes are involved in a lot of the movement in the ring, including the most basic maneuver of bouncing off of them.

HITTING THE ROPES

You will learn that a move commonplace in virtually every match can be much more painful than it looks. Soreness and black and blue marks around the rib cage are common as you grow accustomed to bouncing back and forth. There are several different ways of hitting the ropes depending on your comfort level:

1) Hit the ropes by leaning in with the right side of your body. Go in on your right side with your weight on your right (forward) foot and left (rear) leg leaning into the ropes to show leverage (**1a**). Pivot with your left foot and charge forward (**2a**). Your first step off the ropes should be with your left foot (**3a**). You could also pivot off your left foot before charging forward if that feels more natural.

2) Head toward the ropes just like above (**1b**) but square up so your back bounces off the ropes (**2b**) and then charge forward (**3b**). One advantage to this technique is that you have better vision coming off the ropes and save yourself from some unwanted rib pain.

Regardless of which technique you use, take long strides to show power. Remember the idea is that the ropes are sling-shotting you, so your steps should show that. You can raise your non-pivot leg when hitting the ropes to help generate more momentum. If executed properly, the ring ropes will snap when you bounce off them.

TIP

Regardless of the style used, your right arm should be draped over the top rope and your right hand should always loosely clutch the top rope while in the process of bouncing off. This way, you have some control in terms of where you fall and land if the top rope were to break. Without that grip, you could potentially end up somewhere in the second row of seats!

A good beginning exercise is to stand near the ropes and practice bouncing into them to grow accustomed to leading in with the right side of your body as well as draping your hand across the top rope.

A small skip isn't bad if an adjustment must be made, which can happen if you're not accustomed to the size of the ring, but wrestlers shouldn't stutter-step into the ropes because that destroys the illusion of being thrown into them.

TIP

Do not spin around on your approach and back into the ropes from a few feet away.

Hangman—*n.pr A maneuver where the wrestler catches his head between the top and middle ring ropes.*

WHAT YOU MAY NOT KNOW

Ring ropes can cause major injuries if too loose or too tight. An accident led to Mick Foley losing a sizeable portion of his right ear in March 1994 during a match against Leon "Vader" White while both were in World Championship Wrestling. Foley tried to perform a **hangman.** The ropes had too much tension, leading to Foley suffering major damage to both ears. Foley's right ear was torn almost completely off while his left was badly damaged and needed 12 stitches to repair. Foley actually wrestled for two more minutes, leading to his right ear falling off when countering a Vader blow with one of his own. Foley's right ear was placed on ice but couldn't be reattached. In his bestselling autobiography *Have a Nice Day*, Foley recounted what happened during an encounter with his nurse at the hospital.

"She turned to me and with the enquiring eyes of a child said, '[Translated] Isn't wrestling all fake?'"

It isn't. The incident also added to Foley's lore as one of the wildest performers in grappling history.

RING TALK

I wouldn't be hobbling today if I had been able to work in the new ring I purchased in March 2005 for my World League Wrestling promotion.

I used to work in old boxing-style rings that were 24 square feet and as solid as any floor you've ever stood on. It's the way a lot of rings were in the early 1960s. They were made that way on purpose so when the boxers moved around the ring, they would not have any spring under their feet so they would not risk twisting an ankle or knee. They just moved around on the hard surface.

My new ring has a surface consisting of two-by-10 and two-by-12 pine wood boards covered by a mat. Pine is a soft wood that can take a lot of flexing rather than breaking. Underneath the pine are seven bars going across to hold them up. And right below those are four more bars called catcher bars. *In case something breaks, the wood will go to the catcher bars and stop you from falling all the way to the floor.*

The ring cost $5,000 and takes roughly 30 to 40 minutes to assemble. For those who want a ring but can't afford spending that much money, the most standard ring uses eight sheets of ¾-inch plywood for flooring with a large spring underneath the middle of the mat. But I caution you that all of the action [i.e., bounce] in that ring comes from the middle of it. The problem with it is that you're constantly breaking the plywood.

—Harley Race

TURNBUCKLE WHIP

If you are the one doing the whipping from turnbuckle to turnbuckle (**1**), control your opponent (**2**) until even with the neutral corner before releasing. That way, it appears as though you are actually whipping your opponent.

The wrestler being whipped should begin spinning toward the turnbuckle several feet before impact. Plant your left foot and pivot so your right side is turning to the left. When your back is to the turnbuckle, plant your right foot, jump backward into the turnbuckle, and try to hit it at shoulder-blade level (**3a**). You won't feel as much of a jolt that way. Use your right hand to reach across for the top rope on the left side of the turnbuckle when guiding yourself in for impact.

Bret "The Hitman" Hart was a master at running chest-first into the turnbuckle. The key is hitting the turnbuckle in the mid-chest area with your arms at your side (**3b**). You can also use this approach if your opponent releases you too close to the turnbuckle and you don't have time to turn.

Another option is leaping back-first into the buckle, which adds a more powerful visual on impact.

3a

3b

BUMPS

TIP

Before you begin, purchase heel cups to place in your wrestling boots to help soften the shock of bumping. The heels are not accustomed to this type of pounding and will become bruised and sore when beginning to learn basics bumps.

TIP

Reaching for the floor while falling could result in broken wrists upon landing.

Unless you're the second coming of Rikishi or Andre the Giant, bumps are a part of every match. That makes knowing how to fall without getting hurt so important.

BACK BUMPS

The most basic kind of bump is known as the *back bump*. Here are several different approaches:

Back Bump 1

Grab the middle rope, squat **(1),** and fall backward **(2).** Avoid sitting into the bump. Have your chin tucked in and land predominantly flat on your back/shoulder blades with the pelvis slightly up. Your feet should remain flat on the mat so you don't look like a spider on its back. Your palms should slap the mat at the same time as the landing to help amplify the bump's impact.

Slapping the mat also helps distribute the impact of the fall and actually does lessen the force on the torso.

Back Bump 2

This version requires three people. Wrestler A should be on his hands and knees. Wrestler B should stand facing Wrestler C, who should have the back of his knees next to the torso of Wrestler A **(1).** Wrestler B then shoves Wrestler C over Wrestler A, causing C to take a back bump **(2).** When first doing this drill, Wrestler C should keep his arms folded over his chest. Once comfortable, Wrestler C can use his hands to amplify the sound of the bump **(3).**

The purpose of this drill is to keep the wrestler from developing bad reaction habits while learning to take a bump.

Back Bump 3

Wrestler A walks to the center of the ring (**1**) and then propels himself to the canvas to take a back bump (**2**). Although relatively simple, the key to this drill is practicing hand placement (**3**) to amplify the sound of the bump as well as making sure the landing is correct.

HANDSTAND BUMP

This is the next step after becoming comfortable with back bumps. The wrestler leans forward into a handstand and carries the momentum into a flat landing (**1, 2**). You need to keep your chin tucked and pelvis slightly arched like a standard bump (**3**). Your feet should land in a comfortable position (**4**) at no wider that shoulder length and not get caught under your body or you risk a sprained ankle or knee.

Heavier trainees may struggle with this exercise. Someone too big to safely take this bump can still practice with the help of two fellow trainees. The wrestler taking the bump should begin doing a handstand. The two assistants should each take one leg and help him flip over.

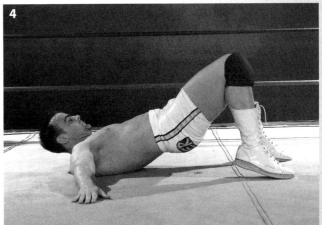

FRONT BUMP

Things start to get more difficult with this bump. Stand in the corner of the ring, step forward, and flip over to land on your back.

The key to this bump—and avoiding a potential neck injury—is remembering that the body will follow the head. Therefore, keep your head up before flipping into this bump.

SNAP MARE

Wrestler A stands in front of Wrestler B. For beginners, Wrestler A should reach back to secure the head of Wrestler B in his hands **(1)**. Wrestler A steps forward with his left foot while bending the right knee. That ensures Wrestler B's head and torso will not crack against Wrestler A's knee. In that same motion, Wrestler B flips himself over the right shoulder of Wrestler A **(2)** and lands like in the standard wrestling bump **(3).** Wrestler A should not apply pressure to help with the flip but instead concentrate on guiding Wrestler B's landing. Wrestler A should try to keep his left hand under Wrestler B's head to make sure the bump goes smoothly without the back of the head snapping off the mat **(4)**. Wrestler B should still keep his chin tucked as with all bumps. Wrestler B also should keep his head up before getting snapped.

Although also used during matches, this maneuver serves as an excellent practice bump.

LEG SWEEP

This is an impressive-looking bump that can be derived from Back Bump 3. As Wrestler B charges forward, Wrestler A drops to one knee **(1).** Wrestler B then does Back Bump 3 as Wrestler A feigns knocking his legs out from under him by moving his arms in a swinging motion **(2, 3).**

COLLAR-AND-ELBOW LOCKUP

This is considered one of the most basic moves in wrestling and is a staple in the starting action of a match.

Wrestler A's left hand should be placed on the back of Wrestler B's neck. Wrestler B should do the same to Wrestler A. Wrestler A's right hand should go on the crook of Wrestler B's left arm and vice-versa **(1)**. The wrestlers should step forward with their left foot and lock up simultaneously with an up-and-down arm motion.

Sounds simple, right? But there are some important nuances to a professional lockup. Don't bring your hands in from too high an angle for the lockup, because it increases the chances of accidentally hitting your opponent in the face. Stand close to your opponent so you're not reaching to where your posture is negatively affected.

Inexperienced wrestlers may sometimes crack heads when leaning in for the lockup. To prevent that from happening, always enter with your head up and angled slightly to the right of your opponent's head. You can place your right hand on the left shoulder/chest area of your opponent to prevent a head-to-head collision.

Make sure to keep a healthy distance from your opponent and keep your chin up so fans can see the struggle on your face as you jockey for an advantage. The collar-and-elbow should look like a struggle for dominance and leverage. This might mean starting a bit stiff with your opponent before loosening your grip.

The lockup serves as the first in a series of chain moves that can be executed, like a snap mare or headlock. By keeping your heads close, you and your opponent can convey spots (i.e., moves) to each other without the fans being able to see. The lockup is rarely used after the midway point of a match and never when going to a finish.

TIP

Put yourself in the position of the fan. Don't let the fans say, "I knew that was going to happen." Try to stay a step ahead by changing things up every match.

1

There is a psychology involved in the collar-and-elbow. You and your opponent shouldn't immediately charge each other to lockup as soon as the bell rings. In most cases, there should be a feeling-out process involved.

An example of this is when Ric Flair feigns a lockup and instead puts his hands to his head and screams his trademark, "Whoo!" Other tactics include going for a leg sweep as your pre-warned opponent gets out of the way or touching hands like a battle for the best grip before locking up.

HEADLOCKS

One of the most basic ways to start a match after the collar-and-elbow is with a headlock. There are several different varieties of headlocks that allow a wrestler to segue into other maneuvers.

STANDING HEADLOCK

Wrestler A should use his left arm to pull Wrestler B's head toward the left side of his upper body while using his right arm to knock away Wrestler B's left arm (1). Wrestler A should then lock his hands together to complete the hold, with the right wrist covering Wrestler B's mouth (2). That allows Wrestler B to call a series of spots without recognition from fans.

For a standing headlock Wrestler A should keep erect posture and not slouch so fans can see the expression of a performer applying pressure on his opponent. Wrestler A's shoulders and feet should be square. Wrestler A also should have his legs split apart with the right foot in front of the left.

Wrestler B needs to keep his head and body close to Wrestler A. If Wrestler B's head begins to slip down or isn't positioned well when the hold is first applied, Wrestler A should pull it up by placing his right hand under Wrestler B's chin. One way to cover that up from fans is to appear to crank on the headlock.

One way for Wrestler B to break the headlock is by throwing his opponent into the ropes. Wrestler B can back Wrestler A into the ropes for that transition. But to keep realism, Wrestler A shouldn't allow himself simply to get walked to the ropes, because Wrestler B isn't in control. Instead, Wrestler B should pull hair or deliver a series of forearms to the back of Wrestler A.

Wrestler A also can revert to the headlock by pulling down Wrestler B's arms using either natural strength or a tug of the hair.

HEADLOCK TAKEOVER

A standing headlock can be turned into a headlock takeover in relatively simple fashion.

Wrestler A, who is controlling Wrestler B, should mumble the word "over" to Wrestler B before beginning the move. Wrestler A should make sure Wrestler B's head is gripped high enough in the headlock before beginning the takeover (1). Wrestler A takes a small step forward with his left foot. Wrestler A then drops to his right knee (2) to prepare to take Wrestler B over his left side and to the mat. Wrestler A should brace himself while performing the takeover by placing his right hand on the mat.

To help with the takeover, Wrestler B should run his arms across the back of Wrestler A and lightly hook his hands on Wrestle A's right side, which helps to prevent Wrestler A from leading with his arms and possibly injuring himself by landing on them as both wrestlers fall. Wrestler B's right hand should be placed above the right hand to help push off and make the bump easier (3). Wrestler B should not try to break the fall with his arm, as it could get broken.

On the mat, Wrestler A should shift his hips so the bulk of his weight is not on Wrestler B's chest (4). Wrestler B should be positioned mostly on his side with shoulders off the mat. Once Wrestler A has shifted his hips through and is in a sitting position with the headlock, Wrestler B should be laying on his back.

To add a little flair to this move after all of the above has been completed, Wrestler B can cradle Wrestler A and roll him back on his shoulders for an attempted pin, getting a one- or two-count before Wrestler A regains his sitting position and control over Wrestler B.

To return to a standing position, Wrestler A and Wrestler B must work together. Because he is holding the headlock, Wrestler A can only use his knees to help get up. Wrestler B also uses his knees but should remain close to Wrestler A so the hold isn't lost. Wrestler A should lean some of his weight on the shoulders of Wrestler B without releasing the headlock. As they go to their left to get up, Wrestler B rolls to his stomach and comes to his knees. Wrestler B can place his hands on the waist of Wrestler A for help in rising smoothly and gracefully.

FRONT FACELOCK

This is predominantly used as a rest hold that allows the wrestlers to catch their breath or call spots for future holds. Wrestler A should wrap his left arm from behind around the neck of Wrestler B and clasp the hold **(1).** Wrestler A's left forearm should fall under the chin of Wrestler B. If it doesn't, the referee should call it a chokehold and call for a break. The referee can help sell this move by checking to make sure the move is applied legally and convey that information to the crowd.

SHOULDER BLOCK

The shoulder block, or standing tackle, is a common move coming off the ring ropes **(1).** Determine which wrestler will take the fall before executing the move. The two wrestlers should collide with their left shoulders making contact and their bodies positioned to the right **(2).** Contact should be made while both step forward with their right feet. The impact can be made even louder if one and/or both wrestlers slap each other across the back on impact. The wrestler who was selected to fall should then fall into a back bump **(3).**

It makes little sense for a larger wrestler to take bumps off standing tackles from a smaller wrestler. The smaller wrestler, though, can gain an advantage on his larger opponent by outmaneuvering him through such tactics as a leapfrog or dropkick coming off the ropes.

HIP TOSS

This maneuver can be done from either a collar-and-elbow position or off the ropes with Wrestler A hip-tossing Wrestler B. Wrestler A places his right arm through the left armpit of Wrestler B. Wrestler B places his right hand on the right hip of Wrestler A in such a position that it can be used to push off **(1).** Wrestler A's right leg should be across the front of Wrestler B to give B something to clear (i.e., a guide). As Wrestler B plants the right hand on A's hip, they should dip slightly together to give a small launch to the hip toss. The wrestlers should be close together. Wrestler B should jump off the balls of his feet, which helps Wrestler A finish executing the toss. For beginners Wrestler A guides Wrestler B's head with his left hand as A lifts B off the ground **(2a).** Once the move is mastered, A can throw B with only one hand **(2b).** Wrestler B should begin the hip toss looking up at the ceiling, because if you go into this move with your head down, you will lack elevation, and there is a chance of landing on the head or neck.

Wrestler B should land on the mat with his chin tucked in and hands slapping the mat to accentuate the impact and disperse the force of the fall **(4).**

When finished, Wrestler B's head and body should be between the legs of Wrestler A or just off to the side.

Wrestler B should not lean into the hip toss. That would likely cause Wrestler A to fall and botch the move.

TIP

Remember—the body must always follow the head!

LEAP FROG

"Groin, groin, gone" is an apt description of what will happen if this maneuver is not executed properly. The move is basic: Wrestler A leaps into the air to jump over Wrestler B, who is running between his legs. Wrestler B must make sure to duck enough to clear Wrestler A's groin area (see page 19, photo 4). Just as important is Wrestler A getting enough height to avoid an unpleasant situation. Wrestler A should remember to jump as if trying to touch his toes or intending to raise his knees as high as he can. That creates a wide berth for Wrestler B to pass under.

FIREMAN'S CARRY

This is an amateur move that translates well into the pro ranks. It also raises the credibility of the performer doing it because of the move's legitimacy.

To execute, Wrestler A drops to his knees and grabs Wrestler B's left arm with his right hand. Wrestler A's left arm then goes behind Wrestler B's left thigh (**1**). Wrestler A uses his right hand to pull down on Wrestler B's left arm (**2**). Wrestler A then uses his left arm to lift Wrestler B. Wrestler B steps into the move and follows through in getting flipped onto his backside (**3, 4**). If Wrestler B doesn't follow through, he will most likely fall on top of Wrestler A and potentially cause injury.

After the move is complete, Wrestler A can hold onto Wrestler B's left arm and easily apply an arm bar (**5**).

ARM LOCKS AND MOVES

There are several moves that focus on the arms and can make effective transition moves out of the collar-and-elbow lockup and into the more complicated maneuvers that build the action of the match.

ARM TWIST

Upon breaking free from a collar-and-elbow lockup, Wrestler A uses his hand to grab Wrestler B's left wrist and begins pulling him down **(1).** Wrestler A then places both of his hands on the opponents left wrist and steps under Wrestler B to "twist" his arm **(2).** The key to the move is that Wrestler A never actually twists Wrestler B's arm but instead gives the illusion of doing so by keeping the latter's arm in the same position while stepping underneath him.

The key to making the hold effective is the selling by both performers. Wrestler A needs to make it appear as though he is applying pressure, while Wrestler B must grimace and act as if his arm is being twisted. From this move, Wrestler A can apply an arm bar or continue twisting until Wrestler B flips over into a back bump.

ARM BAR

A standard arm bar is executed when Wrestler A pins Wrestler B's left arm straight across his chest by placing it under his left armpit **(1)**. Wrestler A's left arm should fall across the biceps/triceps area of Wrestler B's left arm. Wrestler A should use his right hand to grab Wrestler B's left wrist. Wrestler A then places his left hand across his right wrist to cinch the hold on B **(2)**.

STANDING ARM BAR

A standing arm bar out of a collar-and-elbow is executed by Wrestler A wrapping his right arm from the outside around Wrestler B's left triceps. Wrestler A then locks his hands together with Wrestler B's left arm in a straight position **(1).** Wrestler B sells the hold as if his elbow joint were being bent in the opposite direction, which is what would happen if the move were legitimately applied. Wrestler B should start standing on his toes or even bounce up and down to appear to alleviate the pressure and use his right hand to try to "break" Wrestler A's grip **(2).**

ARM DRAG

An arm bar can be used as a hold following an arm-drag takedown. Wrestler B should charge toward Wrestler A with his left arm extended outward from his side at a 90-degree angle (**1**). Wrestler A begins falling backward toward the mat, hooking his left arm under Wrestler B's left arm in the process (**2**). Wrestler B proceeds to flip over Wrestler A. Wrestler A twists to land on his stomach while helping to pull Wrestler B over for a landing (**3**). Wrestler A should place his right hand on the mat to brace himself while spinning over. Wrestler B takes the bump on his back while Wrestler A maintains his hold on B's left arm (**4**). Wrestler A then spins up and applies the arm bar (**5**).

TOP WRISTLOCK

Like the headlock, this move is easy to apply out of the collar-and-elbow position. Wrestler A uses his right hand to grab Wrestler B's left wrist while pulling his left hand away from the back of B's neck **(1)**. Wrestler A then places his left arm across the crook of Wrestler B's left arm while pulling B's left arm back with his right hand **(2)**. Wrestler A completes the hold by locking his left hand across his right wrist and stepping forward to apply pressure **(3)**.

SWITCH-AND-GO BEHIND

From the collar-and-elbow, Wrestler A uses his right arm to push Wrestler B's left arm into the air while moving forward to step behind him (**1**). Wrestler A then clinches his hands around Wrestler B's waist from behind (**2**). Wrestler B can sell the struggle by trying to break Wrestler A's grip (**3**). A switch can be made if Wrestler B shoots his left hand behind the left thigh of Wrestler A while stepping forward and spinning around (**4**). Wrestler B uses his left hand as a guide to pull himself around Wrestler A and complete the switch (**5**).

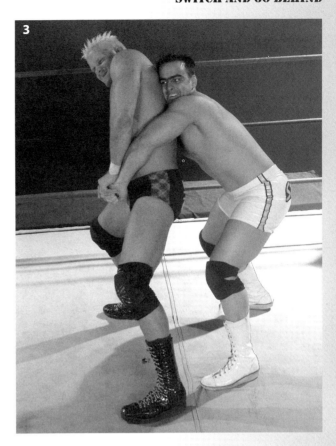

HAMMERLOCK

A move common to schoolyard bullies also has its place in pro wrestling. From a collar-and-elbow lockup, Wrestler A loosens his grip on the back of Wrestler B's neck with his left arm while A moves his right hand to cup the side of B's left elbow (**1**). Wrestler A keeps his grip while then twisting under Wrestler B's left arm and stepping in that direction (**2**). Wrestler A repositions himself behind Wrestler B while bringing his left arm over into a 90-degree angle behind B's back to secure the hold (**3**). Wrestler B should be selling the pain of having his arm trapped behind his back while Wrestler A should sell applying heavy pressure while not actually doing so.

BODY SLAM

Wrestler A bends to shoot his right arm between Wrestler B's legs and places his hand upon the small of B's lower back. At the same time, Wrestler A should place his left arm over Wrestler B's right shoulder so that A's left hand is near B's right shoulder blade **(1).** Wrestler A then lifts Wrestler B into the air so that B's abdominal region is hoisted near A's right shoulder. When reaching the height of the lift, Wrestler A moves his left hand toward the back of Wrestler B's neck. Simultaneously, Wrestler B is placing his right hand on Wrestler A's right thigh **(2).** Wrestler A then slams Wrestler B toward the mat, with A using his left hand to guide B's head and using enough force to ensure B's legs will land heel-first on the mat **(3).** At the same time, Wrestler B is pushing off Wrestler A's thigh to make sure he has a controlled fall. Wrestler B should land as if he were taking a back bump, with his hands hitting the mat to emphasize the impact of the slam **(4).**

DROP KICK

Your athleticism can be displayed through this maneuver. After throwing your opponent into the ropes **(1),** Wrestler A jumps into the air to send both of his feet toward the shoulder area of Wrestler B **(2).** Wrestler B *must* protect himself by placing his right hand underneath his chin to avoid a kick to the face **(2a).** Wrestler B can fall backward just before being kicked to soften the blow. Wrestler A should use Wrestler B's body as a springboard to flip over and land on his stomach **(3).** Some performers are athletic enough to perform this move without having to throw their opponents off the ropes (i.e., a *standing drop kick*).

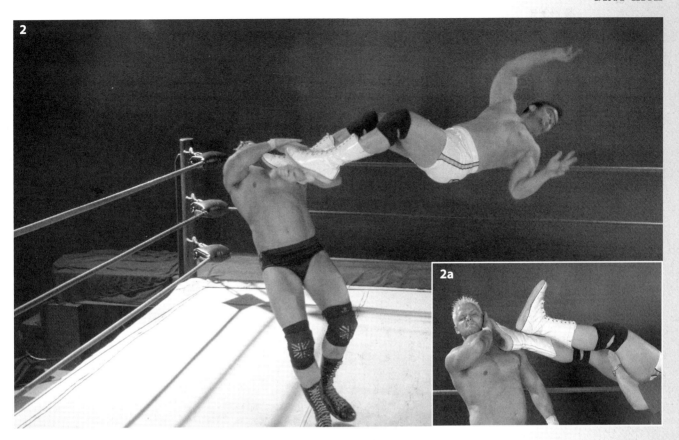

BACKDROP

This maneuver is a sure-fire way to make a crowd pop if executed and sold properly. Wrestler A, who is taking the backdrop, charges toward Wrestler B. Wrestler B ducks and reaches for Wrestler A's thighs **(1)** Reaching for the tops of the shins is also permissible. As Wrestler A places his hands on Wrestler B's back, Wrestler A then springboards himself while receiving a push over from Wrestler B **(2, 3).** Wrestler A can choose to land flat or slightly on his hip, depending on what is more comfortable **(4).** It's important that both wrestlers are relatively close together when performing this move and that Wrestler A does flip completely over. Use an extra mat while practicing.

SINGLE-LEG TAKEDOWN

This is also called a *step-over toe hold*. Wrestler A catches the left leg of Wrestler B **(1),** who proceeds to lose his balance and take a back bump **(2).** Wrestler A can make that happen by using his left leg to "trip" Wrestler B from behind. Wrestler A then places Wrestler B's left leg between his legs by stepping forward so A's left leg is planted just under B's armpit area. Wrestler A then twists Wrestler B's left leg over his left leg and pretends to apply pressure **(3).** Wrestler B can break the hold by using his right leg to push off Wrestler A's chest, causing the latter to take a back bump. Other ways to break the hold are for Wrestler B to gouge Wrestler A's eyes if A bends over toward him.

FIGURE-FOUR LEGLOCK

With Wrestler B on the mat, Wrestler A grabs his opponent's left leg and steps forward to trap it between his legs **(1).** Unlike with a single-leg takedown, Wrestler A should follow through while stepping so that his feet are positioned next to each other with his back to Wrestler B. In the process, Wrestler B's left leg should be wrapped around Wrestler A's right leg from behind **(2).** Wrestler A then places Wrestler B's left foot on top of his right knee so his legs make the image of the number four **(3).** Wrestler A steps over so that his left foot is above the intersection of Wrestler B's left foot and right knee. Wrestler A then drops back to the mat and places his left leg on top of Wrestler B's left foot to give the illusion he is applying pressure **(4).**

The spinning toe hold is performed when Wrestler A continues to "spin" while holding Wrestler B's left leg rather than segue into the figure-four leglock. The key is for Wrestler B to sell that his foot/ankle is being twisted even though Wrestler A actually isn't doing so. Wrestler A is releasing the leg while spinning and not actually apply pressure.

ABDOMINAL STRETCH

Heel—*n A bad guy wrestler whose character should get booed by the crowd.*

Wrestler A stands behind Wrestler B and grapevines his leg over B's left thigh, hooking his toe behind it in the area of B's lower calf. Wrestler A slides his left arm up under B's right armpit and behind B's neck **(1).** Wrestler A also can lock the fingers of his right hand with those on his left to make it appear as though he has more control or leverage **(2).** The illusion is that Wrestler A is stretching the abdominal muscles as well as putting the lower back in a painful position. A **heel** also can cheat by grabbing the ring ropes for increased leverage **(3).**

PINFALL

There are several variations of this standard move. If the match's ending calls for the winner to go over strongly, a decisive pinfall can be scored with Wrestler A placing his legs over Wrestler B's right arm while extending and holding down the left arm with the two performers making chest-to-chest contact (**1**). For a more sadistic-looking cover, Wrestler A can place one of his forearms across the face of Wrestler B à la William Regal's pinfall style in WWE (**1a**).

Wrestler A can use an arm to hook one of Wrestler B's legs and lean back (**2**). As Wrestler A lies perpendicular across the chest of Wrestler B, B should have his arms underneath his body so he is able to push A off of him before a three count is made. Wrestler B's arms should be down by his side with his elbows bent so his hands are cupped on the side of Wrestler A's torso. To break the pinfall, Wrestler B should kick up and shove Wrestler A backward off of him. This should be done forcefully enough that as Wrestler B's legs come down, Wrestler A will be cleared away. For veteran performers, it becomes second nature to kick out at the count of two during a pinfall that isn't the match finish, but there are instances in which you may not get your shoulders up in time. Should that happen, the referee's responsibility is to count to three even though such an ending isn't planned. You may think the backstage heat for a premature match finish will fall upon the referee, but the responsibility falls onto the wrestler to kick out.

TIP

If you're convincingly pinned to end a match, don't immediately bounce to your feet and head to the locker room like nothing had happened. Such an action renders your opponent's victory less meaningful and deflates a crowd. If you lose, appear stunned, surprised, or sell an injury on the way back.

SIDE ROLL

A side roll is a sharp-looking type of pinfall. With Wrestler B on his hands and knees, Wrestler A flips over him (**1**). In the process, Wrestler A uses his left arm to hook B's right arm while placing his right hand behind B's right knee (**2**). Wrestler B then rolls toward Wrestler A and winds up with his shoulders on the mat and legs hooked (**3, 4**).

SUPLEXES

These kinds of throws are impressive and relatively safe. But they do require cooperation between the wrestlers to execute them properly.

VERTICAL SUPLEX

Wrestler A hooks the head of Wrestler B underneath his left armpit **(1).** Wrestler B's left arm is then draped around the back of Wrestler A's neck. Wrestler A grabs the left side of Wrestler B's trunks with his right hand; Wrestler B does the same, except he is preparing to push off Wrestler A's right thigh when the suplex begins **(2a, 2b).** When both opponents are ready, they crouch together and Wrestler A begins to lift Wrestler B in the air so that B's toes are heading toward the ceiling **(3).** Both wrestlers then fall backward to the mat together, with B trying to take as normal a back bump as possible.

There are a number of different variations for this maneuver. You may be coordinated enough to keep your opponent suspended in the air for a long period of time or even walk around the ring while holding him. That gives the illusion that impact is much greater when the suplex is completed.

SNAP SUPLEX

This is done in the same manner as the vertical suplex except much more quickly and at a lower angle **(1)**. Wrestler B basically jumps into his own bump while being guided by Wrestler A, who has to bridge back at a much greater angle than with the vertical suplex **(2, 3)**.

BELLY-TO-BACK SUPLEX

This hold is usually done when one wrestler has another in a side headlock, but it also can be executed when a grappler gets behind his opponent. Wrestler A has his head underneath Wrestler B's left armpit. Wrestler A places his left hand beneath Wrestler B's left thigh **(1).** Both performers squat down together and rise with Wrestler A picking Wrestler B up into the air **(2).** B usually keeps his arm draped around A so the two wrestlers remain in control of the suplex **(3).** After hoisting Wrestler B's torso onto his right shoulder, Wrestler A falls backward to complete the suplex **(4).** Wrestler B should take the brunt of this bump on his shoulders and back as both land simultaneously.

ATOMIC DROP

An atomic drop is easy to apply from the belly-to-back suplex position **(1).** Instead of falling backward with Wrestler B, Wrestler A instead makes a forward drop while sticking out a bent right knee **(2).** Wrestler B should land on his feet but with his coccyx—the small triangular bone at the base of the spine—appearing to hit Wrestler A's knee to make it seem as though that contact sent a jolt through his spine.

2

CHEATS

TIP

One of the keys to throwing an effective punch is being able to come as close to the face of your opponent as possible without making contact.

Although a heel can be an excellent scientific wrestler, using **cheats** helps separate these bad guys from the babyfaces. Here are several basic illegal moves a heel can use to help maintain his bad-boy credibility.

PUNCHES

One of the keys to throwing an effective punch is being able to come as close to the face of your opponent as possible without actually inflicting damage. You should step into the move to give the impression you're throwing the punch with momentum (**1a**). Wrestler A's blow should be pulled and connect with his knuckles landing on the side of Wrestler B's neck (**2a**). Another style of punch can be thrown when Wrestler A controls Wrestler B by the hair (**1b**). The *pulled* punch should connect with Wrestler B's forehead (**2b**).

KICKS

As with punches, a kick should not make actual contact with your opponent but come close enough so the crowd believes there is impact. You can make your kicks appear more convincing by subtly slapping your leg upon impact. Pulling the kick back in a snapping motion after delivering it also gives the illusion of power.

Use the top side of the boot when kicking an opponent who is on his hands and knees. An example of a kick to a prone opponent is featured below. Wrestler A should be positioned several feet away on the side of Wrester B **(1)**. Wrestler A should then plant his left foot, bending the knee slightly, while drawing back his right leg. The top side of Wrestler A's right boot should land in the vicinity of Wrestler B's pectoral muscle **(2)**.

CHOPS

This move is usually sure to draw a "Whoo!" every time from the crowd. Wrestler A should throw the chop to the upper portion of Wrestler B's chest with his hand turned sideways **(1).** The intent is a glancing blow that will generate a slapping sound to the audience **(2).**

TIP

Some wrestlers strike harder than others, so be prepared!

FOREARMS

Forearms are an effective and safe way to look like you are inflicting damage on an opponent. They also are useful in the confines of a match, because a forearm is legal while punching is illegal. A good wrestler will be able to throw a forearm blow that only grazes the opponent.

For a forearm across the chest, Wrestler A bulls Wrestler B into the ropes or corner turnbuckle (**1a**). Wrestler A pushes Wrestler B's head back, then brings down his right forearm with what should be a glancing blow across B's chest (**2a**).

A clubbing-style forearm can be used across an opponent's back. Wrestler A should make impact with the inside part of his forearm, rather than the bone itself to minimize the damage caused to Wrestler B (**1b, 2b**).

FOREARM UPPERCUT

This move is used a lot by British wrestlers. Dory Funk Jr. popularized it in America.

Wrestler A grabs B's neck with his left hand and takes his right arm **(1)** and swings his arm under Wrestler B's chin, making sure that his forearm smacks Wrestler B's chest **(2)**. Wrestler A continues the motion of the forearm as though he is throwing an uppercut, while Wrestler B jerks backward as though he has been punched in the neck or hit under the chin **(3)**. If thrown correctly, the impact of the forearm hitting the chest of the opposing wrestler makes a very loud popping sound. This move can also be done with the left arm if the wrestler throwing the forearm is left-handed.

EAR CLAP

While facing his opponent, Wrestler A extends his arms and claps his hands together around Wrestler B's head (**1**). The key to making this move effective is Wrestler A getting good volume with his clap and Wrestler B selling the move as if his ears were just boxed (**2**).

EYE RAKE ACROSS THE ROPES

With his opponent in a headlock, Wrestler A should clasp both of his hands under the top rope while keeping control of Wrestler B with his body so that B's head moves toward the rope (1). Wrestler B places his hand between the rope and his eyes to protect his eyes. The two can take several steps while in such a position before Wrestler A pulls back, leading to Wrestler B selling that his eyes were gouged on the top rope.

EYE RIP

From behind, Wrestler A places both his hands over Wrestler B's eyes and motions as if he is trying to rip them out **(1).** Again, the key is Wrestler B selling the move.

THUMB TO THE THROAT

This is a move popularized by the legendary Ernie "The Cat" Ladd. While holding a headlock, Wrestler A turns Wrestler B away from the referee so the ref can't see what is happening. Wrestler A then pulls back with his right thumb clearly visible to drive it into Wrestler B's throat **(1).**

In reality, Wrestler A will being his hand inside to his chest just underneath Wrestler B's chin rather than to the throat itself. As Wrestler B sells the move through choking and coughing gyrations, the referee should argue with Wrestler A about performing such an illegal move. Wrestler A should motion that he was using an open-hand thrust (which is legal) as opposed to a thumb to the throat (which isn't).

HAIR PULL

This move is most effective when performed on grapplers with long locks. Wrestler A grabs a handfull of Wrestler B's hair (**1**) and begins to guide him around the ring (**2**). Wrestler B should have his hands on Wrestler A's hands while this is happening. Wrestler A also can "throw" Wrestler B by his hair toward the mat. What actually happens is Wrestler B controls this bump by propelling himself into the air at the right moment and landing on his stomach-side.

STANDARD CHOKE

Wrestler A places his hand underneath Wrestler B's throat rather than grasping it and begins to pretend to choke. Wrestler B should grab Wrestler A's wrist to help keep the arm in place and sell the fact he is trying to escape the hold **(1)**. Wrestler A should relinquish the choke by forcefully pulling back, which gives the illusion he was applying heavy pressure on Wrestler B **(2)**.

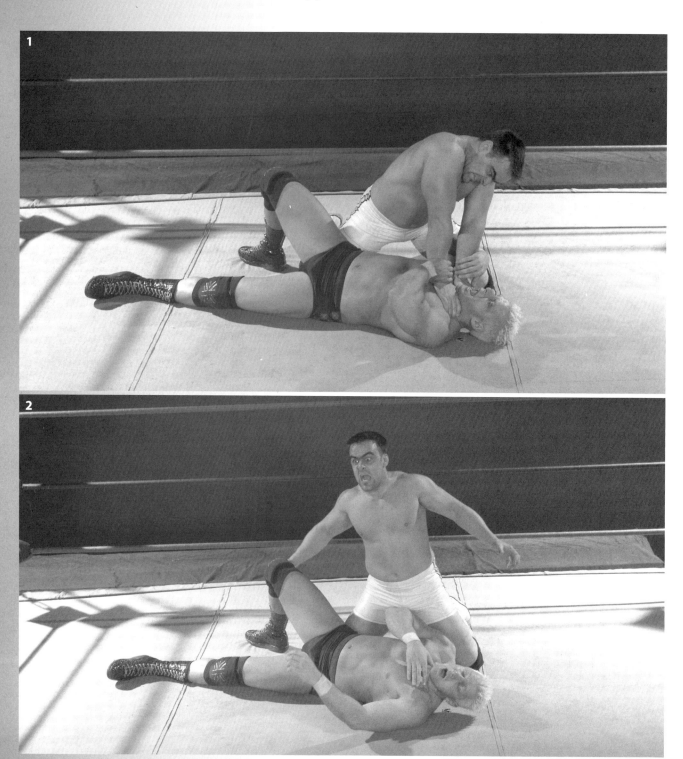

CHOKE ON THE ROPES

Wrestler A grabs Wrestler B's head as if ready to apply a snap mare except that A brings B's body to his side and drapes his right hand under the top rope. Wrestler A then sells that he is pulling down on Wrestler B's head for the choke **(1).** Wrestler B should have his head far enough forward that it's actually his upper chest draped across the top rope. Wrestler B can take a back bump when Wrestler A delivers his final "choke" on the ropes.

RING PSYCHOLOGY

It takes more than just a good physique and knowing the maneuvers to make it in the big leagues of pro wrestling. Being a showman and working the crowd are just as important.

MORE THAN THE MOVES

Imagine the kind of superstar that would be created if a promoter could combine some of the best traits of Hulk Hogan and Dave Batista with the athleticism of a Brock Lesnar.

That's what World Wrestling Entertainment thought it had in Tom Magee. A six-foot-five, 275-pound bodybuilder and weightlifter, Magee appeared poised to become WWE's next major star in 1987 after a tryout match with Bret Hart on a **house show** in Rochester, New York.

But the performer nicknamed the "Mega Man" soon fizzled without ever making a name for himself in WWE, while Hart—a.k.a. "The Hitman"—became one of the top performers in the promotion's history.

The point to the story is that it takes more than a great look to become a pro wrestling star. In fact, it even takes more than the ability to excel inside the ring.

Students who finish their training know the basics. The harder part is understanding **ring psychology.** This is what will have people saying you had a great match and help you achieve the status of being known as a good worker.

There is a reason WWE bills itself as *sports entertainment*. Although physical ability is a must, a wrestler must embrace some of the show business elements of the industry to become a success. You have to have a way to separate yourself from the rest of the guys. Just popping through the curtain with a warmup jacket and getting into the ring is not going to cut it.

While the concept of wrestling characters is handled in the next chapter, there are some universal fundamentals you must know to stand out in a crowd.

House show—*n A non-televised live wrestling event.*

Ring psychology—*n The art of knowing how to elicit a strong fan response by having the ability to call a match in the ring and adjust according to how the crowd reacts.*

RING ENTRANCES

WWE has raised the art of ring entrances to the point that some fans seemingly enjoy them as much as the matches. The sound of the opening chords from a wrestler's theme music—most of which is now specifically developed by WWE for its performers—can drive a crowd into a frenzy with a Pavlovian-like response.

People hear a certain kind of music, and they get geared up before they even see the wrestler, which makes things easier. Smoke, pyrotechnics, and even messages displayed on giant video screens inside the arena are now a given for almost every WWE superstar. Streams of fire shoot from the corners of the ring when Glen "Kane" Jacobs symbolically raises and lowers his arms. Bill Goldberg spewed smoke when storming through a pyrotechnic display in WCW. And graphics on the video screens contain a countdown indicating when Chris Jericho is heading toward the ring accompanied by his theme song, "Break the Walls Down."

You shouldn't expect that same kind of elaborate setup from an independent promoter. Considering the shoestring budgets by which most groups operate, the best you can hope for is a decent sound system in the arena. But that doesn't diminish the importance of the ring entrance when it comes to capturing the crowd's attention.

You have to understand that your wrestling persona starts as you head to the ring. Some guys jog; some do high-fives with the fans; some come through the curtain, pause with their hands on their hips, and look into the crowd hoping to make fans think they're pompous jerks.

There are many different ways to do it. It will take time, but try doing something different from everyone else to distinguish yourself.

There are some universal standards with ring entrances. A male wrestler should never enter the ring between the middle and bottom ropes. That is traditionally reserved for female performers and/or "little people."

RING TALK

I generated so much heel heat during some of my entrances that fans attacked me on two separate occasions en route to the ring.

There is a scar covered by the tattoo on my forearm when I got stabbed in Huntsville, Alabama. I nailed the guy who stabbed me and he went down. I pulled the knife out of my arm, and the cops came running out. I handed them the knife and told them the story.

They said to me, "You're the one that handed us the knife."

I told them, "And I suppose I'm the one who stabbed myself, too?"

The other one was in Winnipeg, Canada. The arena had elevated seats we had to go between on the way to the ring. A guy swung a two-by-four as my partner and I walked to the ring. A police officer was between my partner and me and caught the two-by-four with his nightstick. Of course, that created a mini-riot before we even got to the ring.

—Harley Race

RING TALK

When wrestling as "The Dragon," I came to the ring with a torch and a mouth full of kerosene. As the lights dimmed and a spotlight shone upon me, I climbed to the top turnbuckle and lit the kerosene with a torch while spitting it out to create the illusion of breathing fire.

*There was a little discomfort right after I did the kerosene thing. You would have a residue taste in your mouth and then have to go out and wrestle for 20 minutes. But I never asked off the **gimmick.** I always had a mouthful of*

Gimmick—*n 1) A wrestler's in-ring character. Example: Mark Callaway was known as "Mean Mark" before adopting The Undertaker gimmick. 2) Slang for a foreign object like a chain or brass knuckles used in a match.*

kerosene and didn't want to do any high-fives around the ring. I wanted to get to the top rope and blow out the kerosene as soon as possible.

I was willing to make a physical sacrifice to enhance my wrestling character. As a result, most wrestling fans still know me as "The Dragon" almost 20 years after I began spewing fire in WWE.

Although I admit there was one entrance where I wished I had used better judgment. The only time I had a real problem was in Las Vegas. The ring crew ran out of kerosene and couldn't find any, so someone went to the liquor store and bought some White Lightning, which was 180-proof alcohol. It put out a nice blue fire, but the stuff was toxic. By the time I climbed the top rope, the White Lightning had burned the inside of my mouth like when you bite pizza that's too hot. I had about 10 blisters.
—Ricky Steamboat

PLAYING TO THE CROWD

"I think to build a match, it comes down to being a storyteller. It's not unlike a book or a television show. There's a beginning, a middle, and an end. Whatever your end is, your match has to go toward that."
—Les Thatcher

So you've made it to the ring. Now what?

You may be so excited to start a match that locking up with an opponent happens as soon as the timekeeper's bell rings. But there should be no hurry to get started or perform a bunch of high-risk maneuvers right off the bat.

Building anticipation for contact is the key to drawing fans into a match from its onset.

One of the worst things to do is use bunch of **high spots** in the beginning of a match. If you've hit 40 high-risk moves in the first five minutes, where do you go from there if you have to work a 15-minute match? You have to set the pace and feel out your audience. Also, know where you're going with the match, your limitations, and the limitations of whomever you're wrestling.

There is a time and place to use a move or high spot, a time for the heel to get **heat,** and a time for the babyface to make a comeback. Knowing these times is the hardest and most important part of trying to become a good worker.

Even one of wrestling's most simple maneuvers—the headlock—can capture the audience's interest if both performers effectively sell the move. In one instance, the heel can continue to cheat through hair pulling to retain the hold until the babyface finally gains revenge and works out of it. The babyface also can dominate the heel to a point of frustration that is amplified through facial and body expressions.

TIP

Use the philosophy that "less is more," meaning you should learn how to maximize the effectiveness of holds to draw the crowd into the match rather than stringing together a series of risky or high-flying maneuvers.

High spot—*n A move that carries more weight than most and is usually dynamic, such as Chris Jericho's Lionsault or Rob Van Dam's Rolling Thunder. Although such maneuvers should be used sparingly, some novice wrestlers attempt to string a series of high spots into one match to make amends for a lack of ring psychology. The term* high spot *was first used for a series of moves out of a hold leading to a big bump or bumps and appropriate crowd response, followed by the two wrestlers settling back into that same hold. Today, the current generation may call one single move a high spot.*

Heat—*n What is generated when a crowd is incited by a wrestler. The term* cheap heat *refers to shortcuts taken by a heel to create a response, like swearing or insulting the town where the show is being held.*

THE USE OF BLOOD

Blading—*n When a wrestler intentionally cuts himself with a razor blade or other sharp object to draw blood. This also can be referred to as juicing, gigging, or drawing color.*

Some old-time promoters and wrestlers prescribed to the adage that red equals green. That meant the use of blood translated to increased box-office profits.

Ric Flair, Dusty Rhodes, and Terry Funk are three wrestling legends who enhanced their careers by **blading** on a regular basis. Abdullah the Butcher, The Original Sheik, and "Classy" Freddy Blassie were among the heels known for brutalizing their babyface opponents with foreign objects.

Blood is usually drawn when a performer cuts himself/herself with the edge of a sharp piece of razorblade that is wrapped with athletic tape. But such a practice is *strongly* discouraged on the independent circuit for several reasons, the most important of which is the risk of serious injury. You risk the danger of cutting an artery, permanent scarring, or catching a blood-related disease such as hepatitis if another wrestler also is cut in the ring.

When promotions such as WWE use blood, it is done in a controlled setting, and a physician is backstage to ensure cuts are cleaned properly immediately after the match. You won't have that same luxury with most independent promotions.

The use of blood on the independent circuit also has become cliché with the hardcore wrestling fad winding down. Juicing won't do anything to help you land a job with WWE or any other mainstream promotion.

WHAT YOU MAY NOT KNOW

In earlier generations, one of the hottest debates among wrestling fans centered around whether the blood used by grapplers was real or fake. Many of those same fans were then smartened up on a 1984 edition of *20/20*. Eddy Mansfield, a regional talent who claimed he was being blacklisted by promoters, revealed how wrestlers cut themselves with razorblades to draw blood.

That same *20/20* episode also featured a legitimate confrontation between ABC reporter John Stossel and WWE performer "Dr. D" David Shults. Asked whether pro wrestling was fake, Shults delivered open-handed slaps across both his ears.

"Huh, what do you mean? Fake?" Shults barked at Stossel after the slaps. "What the hell is the matter with you?"

Stossel later successfully won a lawsuit for damages, and Shults only lasted for a short time more with WWE before getting fired.

Although the show exposed pro wrestling matches had predetermined finishes, it had the unanticipated opposite effect upon business. Interest in wrestling actually exploded, with WWE reaping the most benefits.

Your trainer or **booker** will be the one telling you who is going to win or lose your match. That same person likely will help you assemble how the match will unfold.

THE OVERARCHING STORYLINE

The main thread of most wrestling matches is the drama of the babyface versus the heel—the good guy versus the bad guy.

What makes a wrestler a babyface? It is an ability to be the underdog who comes out on top. He/she is the victim of the heel's wrath and cheating ways. The main thing about being a babyface is resonating with the crowd and getting them to empathize with you.

What makes a wrestler a heel? It's more than pulling someone's hair or swearing. It's being a storyteller with facial and body language along with what you do in the ring. What makes you a heel is being outwrestled by the babyface and the frustration that elicits from you. Let that anger build so the people come along with you so when you finally throw that first punch—and it could be five minutes into the match—there's a reason for it.

Booker—*n The matchmaker who oversees storylines, creates the angles, and assigns the finishes to bouts. This person also is sometimes referred to as the* pencil.

RING TALK

I began perfecting how to draw heel heat while wrestling as "Handsome" Harley Race in the 1960s in Verne Gagne's American Wrestling Association.

When you come out to the ring, you'd come out with that ring presence giving off that feeling of domination. I'd walk in front of the ring and point out a very pretty young girl sitting there. I'd pose for her and tell the guy she was with, "Now you see where the 'Handsome' comes from." By the time the match got started, you had a built-in thing that was going to get a big reaction with the very first thing you did.

I would always start with a big high spot. Right at the end of it, a screw up would come and I would take a big bump and slide out of the ring. It would always be in front of the people who I told how great I was. You could imagine the reaction you would get from them. Once you pick that person out and keep playing to him, the field surrounding that person becomes a lot wider and grows to the audience all the way around. At that point, you've pretty much got the people in your hand.

—Harley Race

There will occasionally be babyface versus babyface and heel versus heel matches in promotions that have established characters. But as a beginner, if you and your opponent are dressed the same and work in the same style, fans won't know who to like or dislike, because you're both doing the same thing. That's bad psychology.

Although the storyline may remain largely the same for most matches, it's the different **angles** that keep fans coming back for more.

Angles can extend beyond one match into a longer ongoing tale. There are several different types. One example is the injury angle where one performer "injures" another one. Some injury angles are done to cover

Angle—*n A plot twist that helps build a wrestling storyline. The best angles intrigue the viewer enough to accentuate a feud.*

for a real-life injury that requires surgery or for a wrestler taking a hiatus, such as when John Cena was "stabbed" in a 2004 angle with Carlito Colon so he could take time to film a WWE movie. Other angles try to shock the viewer into thinking an incident is real and falls outside the script, like when Eddie Guerrero's mother faked a heart attack in 2004 to help her son build a feud with John Bradshaw Layfield. There also is the hot-shot angle, where a turn or title change is abruptly booked usually because of panic amid declining business. World Championship Wrestling was guilty of this in 2000 when matchmaker Vince Russo stripped all wrestlers of their titles and started a New Blood versus Millionaire's Club feud.

THE RULES OF THE RING

The formula to most wrestling matches remains relatively consistent. The babyface usually opens with the advantage but loses it because of a mistake or a heel's cheating ways. The babyface eventually makes a comeback, leading into the finish of the bout.

For example, the heel could be a pretty good mat wrestler, but every time he tries something, the babyface is one step ahead and gets the advantage with a headlock or arm drag. This leads to the heel showing frustration. The heel keeps thinking he's going to outsmart the babyface, but time after time, the babyface keeps emerging on top.

Maybe during the time when the babyface is shining, there will be a point when the heel put a stop to it. That paints a picture so that everybody in the arena thinks, "Okay, this is where the bad guy takes over." But out of the blue after a cute little spot, like ducking under a clothesline to hit a dropkick, the babyface is back on top. It again shows the babyface outsmarting the heel.

When it's time for the heel to get heat, he/she does something illegal and dastardly. Finally, after so much frustration, the heel shows the fans the only way he can be on top of a babyface who is one step ahead is by doing something dirty behind the referee's back.

Anything a heel does that breaks the rules usually should be done without the referee seeing it. One flaw with some matches on the independent circuit is when the heels blatantly perform illegal tactics in front of the referee. A heel choking a babyface on the ropes is not bad if the heel is forced to break by the count of five. But don't hold a choke for 30 seconds. That makes fans say, "Why do they even have rules if the heel is going to break them and the referee has no control?"

The same goes for even more extreme maneuvers, like a heel smashing a babyface with a two-by-four in front of the referee. Unless a disqualification is going to be called, that sort of thing should be done behind the referee's back, because the crowd heat then gets transferred to the referee for not doing anything to stop the heel. You can spend 20 minutes building heat, have it transferred to the referee in 20 seconds, and all of your hard work will be gone.

If you do something as a heel to get heat and don't get caught, like placing your feet on the ropes during a pinfall, the heat stays on you. Because although it's as plain as day that everyone in the crowd saw what was going on, the referee didn't and couldn't point a finger at you for breaking the rules.

It's important for wrestlers to respect the role of the referee, or the illusion of the legitimacy of a pro wrestling match is greatly damaged.

You don't want the match to become a street fight, because nothing you do will get over to the crowd. A referee can ruin a match if he's in the way too often or makes stupid calls so the heat goes from the heel to him. A good referee won't allow that to happen.

Also, there is a fine line you should walk when gauging crowd reaction to your match. There are times fans may grow restless with a match that develops slowly or doesn't feature a bunch of high spots at the beginning.

This is extremely important: Don't let the fans completely influence how the bout will unfold!

Do you give the fans what they want? Of course. It's just never when they expect it and want it. Feel the people and listen to them, but when you're in the ring, you have to have a sense that, "This is my house. You'll stand up when I want you up, and you'll sit down when I want you sitting down."

One of the biggest mistakes young wrestlers make is when they hear a couple of people chant, "Boring!" they gear up for a bunch of high spots thinking that will regain the crowd's interest. By doing so, those fans are dictating the match—and they will quickly realize that and influence the tempo until the finish.

Remember that fans at WWE events try the same thing. Take your time and feel confident in your ability to keep the audience involved as the match unfolds. It will pay dividends in the long run and make you a better wrestler.

RING TALK

When I wrestled, I tried to envision beforehand how my matches and angles looked to the fans.

I would try to put myself on the outside looking in. I would go to the top of the arena and see a small ring and play the entire match through my mind. I would tell myself, "This is what I did last week, so this is what the fans think I'm going to do this week." You always try to stay one step ahead because when they can start guessing what's going to happen, why even bother coming? If racing fans could guess who was going to win the Daytona 500, would they bother going?

I would always be happy when I got to the locker room and I could say, "We got them!" because that would keep the fans coming back for more.

—Ricky Steamboat

THE ART OF SELLING

It's easy to make a punch in the face look realistic when someone actually pops you in the nose. But the key to success in professional wrestling is being able to make a maneuver look good without injury being inflicted upon you or your opponent. This is the art of **selling.**

Although heels also do their fair share of selling, it falls upon the babyface to draw sympathy from the crowd. This actually is one of the few areas where a smaller wrestler has an advantage over larger babyfaces, especially if matched against a monster-sized heel.

When the heel gains an advantage during the match, the babyface must be able to convey suffering that causes the fans to feel his/her pain. This is one of the more difficult things to learn during training and will take significant time to develop.

Selling—n What an opponent does when on the receiving end of a maneuver. For example, any opponent caught in Kurt Angle's ankle lock should sell the move by screaming while hooked and limping afterward.

The babyface has to learn how to express pain. One way to know if you're doing that is by looking at a fan sitting in the back of the arena. If you can get that fan to jump out of his seat, it will be like a tidal wave going forward to where those at ringside are doing the same. Sometimes fans in the cheap seats can't see the expression on your face, so you have to translate emotions by using your body.

After working a few matches as a babyface, one way to try to improve physical expression is by wearing a mask. A masked performer has a more difficult time expressing pain because his/her face is covered. Everything has to translate through body language. You will learn how to better sell a kick to the ribs or a punch to the back this way.

WHAT YOU MAY NOT KNOW

Ex-World Championship Wrestling vice president Eric Bischoff was so ardently against masked wrestlers in the 1990s that a slew of Mexican wrestlers, most notably Rey Mysterio and Juventud Guerrera, were forced to lose their hoods. In 2003, Glen "Kane" Jacobs made the transition to wrestling without a mask after having his face covered for six years in WWE.

"It was pretty interesting after spending all those years under the mask," Jacobs told Scripps-Howard News Service. "I had to learn how to use my face to elicit emotion out of the audience. That's basically what we're always going for is getting people to have the most reaction to us, whether they love or hate us. We want them to feel something."

THE COMEBACK

Slip on a banana peel—n A tactic where the heel makes a mistake and the momentum in the bout shifts from the heel to the babyface. This is the beginning of the babyface's comeback.

After being dominated by the heel, the babyface can start a comeback in several ways. The heel could **slip on a banana peel,** meaning a tactic like slipping off the top turnbuckle after the babyface staggers into the ropes. The heel also could miss a major move, like a dive off the top rope.

The babyface also can begin a comeback by fighting up from the bottom. Although the heel remains on the offensive, the babyface begins showing signs of life. This is similar to what Hulk Hogan did when "Hulking up" to begin his comebacks.

The babyface also must do his part by not making the comeback look mechanical. Don't just let out a yell, clench your fist, throw it in the in air, and immediately start your comeback. Try to find a way to build anticipation among the crowd. Throw your fist in the air seven or eight times or let out several yells at the top of your lungs. This helps establish to fans how you respond when the heel has been kicking your butt. This is called **showing fire.**

Showing fire—v Making a comeback seem a legitimate part of the match.

Just before the babyface starts the comeback, the heel should begin begging off. The heel asks the babyface to back off, and the babyface does something to tell everyone he isn't doing that by charging forward. As the babyface begins to regain control of the match, the heel should begin **feeding** the babyface. It's extremely important the heel expresses fear that the babyface is about to win the bout. That plays a key part in drawing fans into the match finish.

Feeding—v The heel's reaction to the babyface as the babyface makes a comeback. This results in selling the comeback and building the anticipation toward the match finish.

There are different ways for the babyface to show excitement over extracting revenge against the heel who cheated to dominate him/her earlier in the match. Several ways to indicate this are by bending over and hitting the mat, throwing your first in the air and letting out a big scream, jumping in the air to touch your toes, or doing a hooch-coo dance around the ring with your arms flailing.

As a babyface, this is your time to shine. Do whatever it takes to get the crowd involved!

THE MATCH FINISH

Shortly after that, you head into the finish of the match. If the babyface is going over strong, the match ends at the peak of his comeback. If the heel is winning, you can turn the tide back after the babyface's comeback by doing a **screw-job finish** like scoring the pinfall with your feet illegally on the ropes.

If that happens, the babyface can exact revenge on the heel until the latter rolls out of the ring and scampers to the locker room. Or the heel could immediately make a quick retreat after winning, leaving a disgruntled babyface in the ring to argue with the referee. Regardless, whoever wins and loses should be sure to express the appropriate response to what happens in the match.

Screw-job finish—*n When a match doesn't have a clear-cut conclusion. Examples include disqualifications, count-outs, or whenever a wrestler cheats and/or needs outside interference to defeat his opponent.*

SELLING YOURSELF

WWE is believed to have received 2,000 to 2,500 videotaped entries to participate in its original Tough Enough *series in 2001. If placed in that same situation, how would you make yourself stand out in such a large field of people who dream of becoming pro wrestlers just like you?*

So much of wrestling is about showmanship—the ability to sell yourself and your storylines. It's about grabbing people's attention and keeping it focused on you. This serves to make you a babyface or heel and helps you catch a promoter's attention. You need in-ring skills, but unless you are blessed with phenomenal athleticism, that won't be enough to help you move up the ranks into the upper echelon of promotions. Good character development, solid interviews, and smart marketing will give you an added edge in getting regular work on the independent circuit and possibly beyond. The more complete package a young wrestler has to offer, the more attractive he or she is to promoters.

Here are some of the elements that will help you down that road.

DESIGNING A CHARACTER

Once you have mastered the basic fundamentals inside the ring, you should look toward creating a character that will help define your wrestling persona. This should be done with the idea of showcasing your uniqueness as well as accentuating your positive skills and features while hiding your negatives.

This is one of the toughest aspects of pro wrestling, because the tendency is to copy gimmicks or aspects of other wrestlers who are already famous. When Steve Austin got hot in WWE, the independent circuit was filled with kids who shaved their heads, grew goatees, got leather vests, and ran around flipping people off. The only reason the gimmick works for him is that it *is* him. It doesn't work for anybody else and mimicking him gets you branded as a cheap ripoff both in and out of the locker room.

A lot of beginning wrestlers begin training with a persona and shtick in mind. But the best time to focus on the performance aspect of professional wrestling is after logging some ring time. This gives you time to see what role you are comfortable playing in front of an audience and what personality aspects you best portray.

Some newcomers will approach their trainer and say, "I've got my gimmick and music picked out." Nine out of 10 times, that gimmick will not fit that particular person. There are independent workers who try to portray themselves as superheroes or sex symbols, and it just doesn't fit.

TIP

Every young wrestler should remember this: Directly copying someone else's character is a recipe for failure.

In their minds, that's who they are. But it's not who they are and won't get them in with the crowd.

"There are some beginners who are trying to fill a gimmick that doesn't need to be filled. I told a kid who was six foot four and who had asked me for advice that he needed to gain about 30 pounds. He said he didn't want to because he wouldn't be able to do his high flying. I said, 'Here's the bad news: There are no six-foot-four cruiserweights.'"
—Les Thatcher

TIP

Figure out what works for you, your body, and your personality. Incorporate it into the character you are developing.

The key to developing a ring persona that is attractive both to promoters and the audience is to find out who you are and be true to that. Most wrestling characterizations are just exaggerated versions of the person doing the performing. For example, Kurt Angle seemed like he would make the perfect babyface performer when first debuting in WWE because he was a 1996 Olympic gold medalist in wrestling. But rather than doing a rah-rah patriot gimmick that worked so well for wrestlers such as "Hacksaw" Jim Duggan and Sergeant Slaughter, it didn't take long for Angle and WWE to figure out that he was best suited as an obnoxious, boisterous heel who could be described as an "ugly American."

"Basically, this is the real-life Kurt Angle," Angle said during a 1999 interview with Scripps-Howard News Service. "It's just turned up about 10,000 notches. I'm proud of what I've done, and I do like to talk about amateur wrestling and the success I've had. For the most part, I'm pretty humble. But here when I speak my mind and then amplify it to such an extent, people say, 'Gosh, that kid is sticking it to me too many times.' What I'm doing is having fun. When I see the reaction, it's quite a treat for me."

Not every performer will find his niche as quickly as Angle did. Dwayne Johnson was miscast as the milquetoast Rocky Maivia upon his WWE debut before morphing into The Rock. Terry Bollea was known as Sterling Golden before becoming Hulk Hogan. Dave Batista was portrayed as the colorless "Deacon" Batista until getting a character makeover. Even Steve Austin flopped as "The Ringmaster" in his WWE debut before developing his Stone Cold persona.

Don't be afraid to fluctuate between being a babyface and a heel. Maybe you have a gift at drawing sympathy from the crowd through facial expressions and body language, but you would never know that if you were always a heel. Such flopping also will help you know how to work a crowd from different perspectives. Finding out whether you are better suited as a babyface or heel will take some time.

Until the mid-1980s, most performers began their careers as babyfaces and gravitated toward being heels. But then came the emergence of babyfaces who were cheered when using mannerisms normally reserved for heels. Today, there isn't a lot of difference between the personalities of the heels and babyfaces.

When first starting, do what you're comfortable with and what comes naturally. You will end up doing better with something you like rather than something you're uncomfortable with. Don't walk to the ring, get the match over with, and come back through the curtain scared half to death. Open up a little bit. Walk to the ring with a little attitude. Tell a person to shut up if that's what feels comfortable.

You can draw from established performers. Many of today's biggest stars were able to take an aspect of someone else's character and tweak it so that it became known as their own trademark. For example, strutting in the ring is fine. Just don't do it in exactly the same fashion as Ric Flair, or you'll turn off the audience.

RING TALK

Early in my career during the 1960s, I had to learn the hard way about developing a character that was bold and unique. I had put together a routine that I felt was strong, so I asked former National Wrestling Alliance champion Pat O'Connor to watch one of my matches. After the match, I sought out Pat to see what he thought.

He said, "I saw Buddy Rogers and Don Eagle. When do I get to see you?"

I was stumped. I didn't get what he was saying. But then I realized that because I was green, I picked up all of these moves and mannerisms from the people I idolized and was putting them out there. As many years as he had been in the business, Pat realized that was the case.

So I kept some of those things I was doing but modified them in a way to make them mine.

—Les Thatcher

Listen to those around you while developing your persona, especially anyone who has achieved a modicum of success in the business. Their advice and observations can give additional and invaluable insight as you polish your character.

Some of wrestling's best gimmicks and nicknames have come from offbeat sources. Austin got his Stone Cold moniker from a description of the temperature of tea made by his ex-wife. Dwayne Johnson probably wouldn't have gotten nicknamed The Rock if his father weren't ex-wrestler Rocky Johnson.

RING TALK

I became known as "Handsome" Harley Race in the mid-1960s after being paired with "Pretty Boy" Larry Hennig, who is the father of the late "Mr. Perfect" Curt Hennig. I was later re-packaged as "The King" after making the jump to WWE in 1985.

Although WWE was refusing to publicly acknowledge title reigns from other promotions at the time, I was shown respect by being billed as "The King" because of my status as a seven-time NWA champion.

—Harley Race

WHAT YOU MAY NOT KNOW

As "Kane," Glen Jacobs has become one of the most successful performers in WWE history. But before being cast as The Undertaker's baby brother, Jacobs bounced around using such lousy wrestling gimmicks as The Christmas Creature, UnaBomb, and Isaac Yankem D.D.S.

"With this [Kane] character, I finally know what I'm capable of doing," Jacobs told Scripps-Howard News Service in December 2003.

Jacobs should consider himself lucky that he managed to avoid the same WWE fate as former tag-team partner Rick Bogner. After Scott Hall and Kevin Nash defected to World Championship Wrestling in 1996, Jacobs and Bogner were recast by WWE as the new Diesel and Razor Ramon, respectively.

The idea was a complete failure, because the audience saw Jacobs and Bogner as frauds. Bogner quickly faded from WWE and then spent the remainder of his career wrestling in Japan before retiring because of a neck injury in 2001.

THE ART OF KAY FABE

Considering how much the secrets of the wrestling industry have gotten exposed after the business boom of the mid-1980s, it would be unrealistic for you to convince every fan that matches are legitimate sporting contests. That is especially true on the independent level, where moves between beginning students are not going to look as crisp as those performed by veterans.

But just because fans realize match outcomes are predetermined doesn't mean you can't help perpetuate the illusion that pro wrestling is real.

For heels, give off that aura of aloofness while you're in the arena without being so rude as to cause a legitimate fight with a fan. That may mean not saying hello when spoken to or refusing to sign autographs. Don't hang out with a babyface opponent in public after a match or get caught traveling to and from the arena together.

This may sound extreme, but these demands are nothing compared to how it was in previous generations. In the 1960s and 1970s, babyfaces and heels rarely rode together or flew on the same airplane, and they never socialized together publicly.

WHAT YOU MAY NOT KNOW

The Iron Sheik and Jim Duggan learned the hard way about babyfaces and heels mingling together. Duggan and Sheik (Khosrow Vaziri) were arrested in May 1987 on drug- and alcohol-related charges while traveling together, which was a major faux pas for two wrestlers who were feuding against each other at the time. The story drew headlines because Duggan was a patriotic babyface while Sheik was portrayed as a Middle Eastern heel. Sheik and Duggan were both fired by WWE, although the latter was re-hired within a year and given a renewed push as if nothing had ever happened. WWE also eventually forgave Iron Sheik and inducted him into its Hall of Fame in 2005.

An effective interview style usually goes hand in hand with a wrestling persona that works. Although it will take time to find your wrestling gimmick, it's never too early to begin trying to practice your oratory skills. **Cutting a promo** is central to success in pro wrestling.

In previous generations, a wrestler who struggled with interviews was pushed as not being able to speak English or would be paired with a manager possessing the gift of gab. But the day of the manager as a mouthpiece has largely passed, which puts pressure on you to deliver.

Ideally, you will be able to cut interviews while being taped by a video camera. You can then replay the interview for evaluation. Audio recordings will suffice, but they don't allow you to watch the physical expression that is vital in the delivery process. Another option is doing the interview in front of fellow trainees or even interacting with them.

If necessary, use a mirror to see how you look when trying to express anger or what your reaction is if someone springs a surprise upon you. Monitor your facial expressions when you talk. You also should listen to your voice to see how you use different levels of tone.

One group exercise, developed by ex-WWE official Kevin Kelly, is to put the names of famous wrestlers in a hat. Draw a name and cut a promo in the style of that wrestler. This takes you out of your comfort zone and allows you to experiment with different types of characterization. It also gets you to think about character development.

Cutting a promo—*n The act of doing an interview. Usually, a wrestler's promo addresses a feud against another performer. This phrase also can be used when one performer addresses real-life problems with another during an on-air interview.*

RING TALK

I devised a drill called "The Gauntlet" while heading a WWE developmental territory (Heartland Wrestling Association) in 2001.

We would put someone behind the desk in my office and line up the other wrestlers outside the door. Each person who came through the door would say something unscripted to the person behind the desk. The person behind the desk would have to play off it and see how far he/she could take it. Then the next person would come in after hearing what was going on in the office. That person could either take that in a new direction or do something different, and the person behind the desk had to go with them. It was a mental exercise.

—Les Thatcher

There is no uniform way to deliver a wrestling interview. Performers such as Dwayne "The Rock" Johnson, Mick Foley, and Nick "Eugene" Dinsmore are able to effectively intersperse humor into their interviews. Some grapplers incorporate catchphrases that can have an entire audience chanting along with approval.

In many cases, there are only minor distinctions between babyface and heel interviews. "Stone Cold" Steve Austin gained recognition as one of the industry's greatest interviews by talking largely about himself rather than the opponent he was facing. Bill Goldberg and Dave Batista reached stardom with a primitive interview style that conveyed intensity primarily through body language. Every interview style should get across the point the wrestler wants to make to bolster his own character and the storyline he's involved in.

You should try to tailor everything toward real life because people can identify with that. Don't say unbelievable things like, "I want to win this one for the fans," after your opponent has done reprehensible things against you. Fans understand that you want to kick this guy's butt for yourself.

RING TALK

During my time as the National Wrestling Alliance champion, I was so busy traveling that I often entered matches against performers from other regional territories without much knowledge of their current storylines and angles. Because of limited television syndication for wrestling promotions during the 1960s and 1970s, I sometimes stepped into the ring not even knowing the performer I was facing. But my interviews were known for an intensity that allowed my real-life toughness to shine through while also piquing fan interest to see the NWA title being defended.

Probably the most effective promo I did was generic. It would fit just about anybody. I would go through the accolades of whomever it was I might be wrestling. I'd talk about how great they were and how close they'd come to winning the title before.

I would wind it up by saying, "But you people have to know that the greatest wrestler on the face of God's green earth is going to be appearing in that ring tonight, and no matter who it is on the other side, that greatness will carry me through." That used to get a lot of heat with a lot of people.

—Harley Race

Like when defining your wrestling persona, one of the most difficult things to avoid when perfecting an interview style is blatantly copying the material and delivery style of established performers. You don't want to be copying the catchphrases of performers such as Chris Jericho or Scott "Raven" Levy word for word. You can take bits and pieces of people from here and there and add an original twist.

TIP

Be comfortable with the things you're saying. Be your own worst critic.

MARKETING YOURSELF

Backyard wrestling—n *A genre in which untrained wrestlers try to perform their own matches at home without having received the proper training. This style is strongly discouraged, as wrestling without being taught by an experienced trainer can lead to injuries and even death.*

Don't fall into the *Tough Enough* trap. The majority of wrestlers dreaming of a career in WWE or any other major-league promotion have little chance of getting booked simply by sending in a videotape of interviews and matches held in a non-professional setting.

In fact, WWE throws away all tapes of what is known as **backyard wrestling.**

Only after spending time working on the independent circuit will you find yourself ready to land a spot with an elite training school, score dates with promotions in another part of the country, or even get signed to a WWE developmental contract.

You may be tempted to assemble a highlight tape chock full of high spots. But that isn't what top promoters care to see when deciding whether to hire you. They are more interested in how crisp you look while performing basic maneuvers. That shows you have the ability to put on a quality match with other performers with whom you might not necessarily be familiar.

WHAT YOU MAY NOT KNOW

Matt and Jeff Hardy are examples of self-taught wrestlers who would practice acrobatic maneuvers while training on trampolines in the backyard of their North Carolina home. But in a 2001 interview with Scripps-Howard News Service, Matt Hardy spoke out against the backyard-wrestling craze that flourished in the late 1990s when WWE, WCW, and Extreme Championship Wrestling were especially popular among young adults and teenagers.

"We did stuff like we saw on TV in a regular match," Hardy said. "We would do body slams or superplexes or throw somebody off the ropes and give them a clothesline. It's so bad today because kids are emulating the extremes, like going through flaming tables or jumping off ladders. It's kind of grown out of control.

"Anybody who wants to get into wrestling should go to a wrestling school and do it the right way. Start small with independent promotions, meet people, and make connections like that."

Extreme-style wrestling won't catch the eye of many promoters, especially when there is little fundamental grappling involved. But such a style can lead to permanent scars and physical damage, which is strongly discouraged.

Smaller wrestlers dreaming of stardom by using a high-flying style also need to have a solid foundation. Rey Mysterio is considered one of the most athletically gifted athletes in WWE history, but after a series of knee injuries forced him to tone down his approach, Mysterio's knowledge of the basics allowed him to successfully change his repertoire of moves.

A wrestler who only does high spots will eventually bore an audience, because fans eventually won't buy their matches as realistic. A high-risk style also results in a higher chance of injury, especially for larger performers trying to perform moves generally reserved for **cruiserweights.** Even the best cruiserweights eventually get grounded because of the wear and tear of such moves.

Extreme-style wrestling—*n Matches involving such props as barbed wire, thumbtacks, staple guns, and the like.*

Cruiserweight—*n A smaller performer who generally weighs 200 pounds or less. Cruiserweights usually wrestle at a faster pace with more flying maneuvers than their larger peers.*

"No matter what you see on WWE television, when they run a weeklong training camp, they look for whether you can lock up properly, tell a story, and are you physically in good shape. I've also told my students that if WWE offers you $1 million without having to learn the basics, forget everything I've taught you and move on with your life."
—Les Thatcher

In compiling your videotape, show that you know where the camera is, like experienced performers do, to better convey your moves and facial expressions to the audience watching on television. This is especially true if you're going to take a high-risk bump and put your body in jeopardy. Don't take a spill over the top rope if you know a camera isn't in position to capture the spot.

You can practice knowing how to perform for the cameras even if there aren't any there to tape your match. During a training session, place a broomstick 10 feet away from the ring to represent a camera and try to have most of your moves positioning your face in that direction.

Glossy publicity photos are effective to submit along with a video-tape/DVD if you have an impressive look or physique. Even something unique about your appearance can be used to your advantage. For example, the hair all over Matt "A-Train" Bloom's body reminded WWE executives of George "The Animal" Steele, and that helped lead to him getting hired by the promotion.

Most performers on the independent circuit are not going to have the same kind of lavish costumes as their WWE counterparts, so don't try to wear something that will pale in comparison. Standard wrestling tights and boots, which can be purchased via the Internet, are fine for promotional photos.

Also, buy gear that accentuates your positives rather than negatives. For example, some wrestlers wear bicycle shorts thinking it better emphasizes the size of their legs when standard black trunks actually do a better job of doing so.

A personal website can be used to allow a promoter to view match footage, interviews, and any media coverage the wrestler has received.

TIP

About 70 percent of your moves should be done facing the camera. But also don't forget that there is a live audience that you have to keep interested in your bout.

WORKING UP THE LADDER

There isn't just one road to stardom when it comes to professional wrestling. Many of the industry's top stars took diverse paths in reaching the top.

Performers such as Dwayne "The Rock" Johnson and Kurt Angle defied the odds by spending only a short amount of time in WWE developmental territories before landing with spots on the regular roster. Chris Benoit and Eddie Guerrero had success in Japan before getting their break in the United States. Even "Stone Cold" Steve Austin and Hulk Hogan bounced around regional territories until landing with major promotions.

As of summer 2005 there is only one WWE developmental territory (Ohio Valley Wrestling in Louisville, Kentucky) up and running at this time. Although much of OVW's top talent has signed with WWE, the school also offers training for non-contracted talent. For more information, visit www.ovwwrestling.com or write Ohio Valley Wrestling LLC, Attention: Danny Davis, 4400 Shepherdsville Rd., Louisville, KY 40218. A training center is being planned in Georgia.

The best hope for you to make a full-time living in today's business is to work for a series of independent promotions. Most promoters run shows on weekends. Few are able to draw large enough crowds to justify running on a weekly basis, which means you should try to build a calendar working for various groups.

You should be trying to establish a name and build a video library if those groups have a television product. Such footage could help lead to opportunities with bigger independent promotions in the United States, a shot at touring overseas, or even landing a spot with a WWE developmental territory.

But in reality, you may never advance beyond the independent circuit, let alone receive regular bookings, unless proving yourself as a talented hand. Smaller performers will find it especially difficult to reach the big time.

But even if you're lacking in height, you might not be lacking in job

RING TALK

I try to address some of the realities of the business as soon as a student joins my World League Wrestling training program. First off, I ask what their goals are in wanting to become a wrestler. If it's a 180-pound kid, I level with them and tell them what I think their odds are of going any further than just working on one of my shows. Ninety percent of the people, the odds of them being able to move on to WWE are slim to none. The odds of being able to move on to a Japanese organization are a lot better if they have three things: Heart; a willingness to put your body through what it's going to take to do this, which is the most important thing; and some size.

If you have that physical structure and the heart, the odds of going there are much greater, although it's still way below 50 percent. Once you've proven yourself in a foreign organization, WWE then starts taking a closer look at you. Almost all of the kids are going to go no further than independent promotions.

—Harley Race

opportunities thanks to the proliferation of independent promotions operating in North America in the aftermath of wrestling's boom period in the late 1990s and early 2000s. Many training schools run shows featuring their students or have connections with other promoters to help talent get booked elsewhere.

But you shouldn't enter the independent circuit blindly, especially in states without athletic commissions to regulate the promotions. Before accepting any booking, you should weigh the following factors.

SAFETY

Even in a promotion the size of WWE, performers are not covered by medical insurance (although the promotion traditionally has paid for the surgeries of performers who are injured while wrestling). You likely will have to rely on personal medical insurance if injured or risk what can be staggering medical costs for an injury suffered while wrestling.

The wise wrestler will make sure the working conditions are acceptable before agreeing to the booking. Know how safe the ring is and whether you are booked to face an experienced/competent performer. Working against a fellow student you trust for another promoter is one way to protect yourself.

PAYOFFS

There isn't a standard payoff for independent wrestlers, but it's safe to say you won't be getting rich when first starting. If you're wrestling for the person who trained you, expect to earn between $0 to $25 because it's part of the learning process. More established performers are going to earn more. Even when first booked by another independent promoter, you may make little more than enough money to cover your transportation costs.

One ploy among some trainers who promote shows is to make their students sell tickets if they're booked to wrestle. That is considered an acceptable practice, although be wary if selling the most tickets, rather than talent, earns someone a spot in the main event.

Be wary of the independent promoter who said he will handle the financial arrangements of your booking. That promoter may reward himself/herself with a booking fee, which can constitute what could be a significant percentage of your earnings without him/her ever having done anything in the ring.

"Back when I was first starting in the 1960s, the promoters had what they called a guarantee. It varied from territory to territory. The standard $25-per-night guarantee was real common throughout the industry. But one time when I was working for [Tennessee-based promoter] Nick Gulas, I drove from Memphis to wrestle in Cleveland, Tennessee, and then drove back to Nashville. I made $7. It cost me nearly triple that in gasoline. By the time you count food as well, I probably came out –$30 or –$40 for the evening."
—Harley Race

RING TALK

My first payoff when I began wrestling out of Boston in 1960 was $12—and that included transportation. But my creativity allowed me to make some additional cash on future shows. Where I got enterprising my first two years in Boston was when the promotion began paying a wrestler to drive everybody. I had a decent car because I was into hot-rodding, so I would take a carload of wrestlers. On top of my $15 or $20 payoff, I would pick up an extra $15 or $20 in a transportation stipend.

At age 19, I would make $150 a week, which in 1960 and 1961 was a lot of money for a young guy. My friends back home were making about $75 a week. Back in the old days, we also would charge two cents a mile from guys I would drive. But you needed a new car every two years, and you had better be setting aside money for that.

—Les Thatcher

WHAT YOU MAY NOT KNOW

Even landing a spot with WWE doesn't guarantee riches. The *Wrestling Observer Newsletter* reported that performers from WWE's *Tough Enough* competition in late 2004 who the promotion had interest in signing to developmental contracts were offered deals worth $39,000 a year. One aspiring performer in WWE's Ohio Valley Wrestling territory in Louisville, Kentucky, had to wait tables at a local restaurant earlier that year to make ends meet.

Most WWE performers are given contracts that contain what is known as a **downside guarantee.** That wrestler can then make significantly more money through appearances on pay-per-view shows, merchandising agreements, and working at house shows. But the contract protects WWE from a financial standpoint in case a wrestler gets injured or no longer fits into the promotion's storylines.

Downside guarantee—*n A contract that promises a minimum annual salary.*

PRACTICALITY

Because of the physical risk of injury inherent in every match, you should weigh the above factors along with the importance of the booking before opting whether to accept it. If you have a full-time job, it probably isn't worth using a vacation day to wrestle for a small-time promoter in a match that won't significantly advance your career.

Sometimes a change of residence is necessary to further your wrestling, especially if the independent promotions in your area provide poor payoffs or a minimal chance for career advancement. The only way to get better is to work with better performers, including those who may have slightly different styles. You can get into a rut working against the same opponents over and over or having to carry lesser opponents on a regular basis. Over time, your skills are going to diminish.

TIP

You can wrestle the same opponent a million times, but that doesn't teach either of you anything beyond what both of you already know.

APPENDIX

Professional wrestling has a language all its own. The *carny* spoken among performers dates back to the time when wrestling matches were held at carnivals. Grapplers learned a secret way to communicate amongst themselves to protect the inner workings of the business, especially from inquiring fans. Wrestlers would use a variation of Pig Latin combined with terms unique to the industry, which is a practice still done by some performers today. The term *kay fabe* is used to describe that exclusionary process.

The following terms should help you blend in more quickly inside a locker room as well as understand what some of the veterans and promoters are saying. But the aspiring wrestler also should know that acting too wise about the business around veterans will cause them to lose respect for you in the locker room. As a result, you may get *kay fabed*.

Wrestling terminology doesn't end with this list of definitions. In fact, ex-WWE grappler B. Brian Blair wrote a 97-page book called *Smarten Up! Say It Right* that is chock full of more insider expressions. Blair said at one time he was such a staunch believer in "protecting the business" from regular fans that he would legitimately try to fight those who said matches weren't real. But Blair, who worked as one half of the Killer B's tag-team with "Jumping" Jim Brunzell in the 1980s, changed his mindset after pro wrestling became regarded as entertainment rather than legitimate athletic competition during the 1990s.

"I think the smarter the fan becomes, the closer they become to the business," Blair said in a 2001 interview with Scripps-Howard News Service. "All the people that get on the Internet buy tickets. Why not have everybody like that? It's good for business.

"I was the first one to argue that Vince [McMahon] was going to kill the business when he exposed it in the 1980s. [Hulk] Hogan was the one who told me, 'No, it will be great for business.' I didn't believe it at all. They were right."

GLOSSARY

Angle—*A plot twist that helps build a wrestling storyline. The best angles intrigue the viewer enough to accentuate a feud.*

Babyface—*A good-guy wrestler whose character is intended to be cheered on by the crowd.*

Backyard wrestling—*A genre in which untrained wrestlers try to perform their own matches at home without having received the proper training. This style is strongly discouraged, as wrestling without being taught by an experienced trainer can lead to injuries and even death.*

Blading—*When a wrestler intentionally cuts himself with a razor blade or other sharp object to draw blood. This also can be referred to as* juicing, gigging, *or* drawing color.

Blowing up—*When a wrestler gets exhausted during a match due to poor conditioning. That wrestler's opponent will have to either slow down the pace or end the match prematurely.*

Booker—*The matchmaker who oversees storylines, creates the angles, and assigns the finishes to bouts. This person also is sometimes referred to as the* pencil.

Bump—*The fall that a performer takes.*

Burying—*When a wrestler is made to look bad through an embarrassing angle or series of losses. Such* burials *can stem from punishment for a real-life incident, like an embarrassing arrest or behavior-related problem, or even lead to the firing of that performer. When the industry had multiple promotions and telecasts were shown only on a regional basis, a wrestler was often buried before jumping from one territory to the next to help keep the performers who were remaining in the territory strong.*

Broadway—*Any match that goes the time limit. A true broadway is considered a match that lasts for 60 minutes or more.*

"In the early part of the 1900s, many wrestlers were booked from the New York office, and the finishes were telegraphed to the promoters in each city. Broadway was part of the code used so that the telegraph operators didn't know what the meaning of the message was. Cadillacing meant you were going over [i.e., winning] and each wrestler had a code name. For example, 'Red Dog and Yellow Belly go broadway.'"
—Les Thatcher

Carny—*The language spoke by wrestlers to protect the business from the outsiders. Carny is similar to Pig Latin. The phrase originated in the carnivals, which held legitimate and staged wrestling matches through the 1960s.*

Carrying an opponent—*The act of a veteran performer leading an inexperienced opponent through a match by calling almost all of the moves.*

Cheats—*Shortcuts generally used by heels to draw heat from the crowd.*

Comeback—*When a wrestler recuperates from being beaten down. The* Superman *comeback refers to a wrestler not selling his opponent's moves while regaining an advantage. Hulk Hogan was well known for his Superman comeback, shaking and quaking while being pummeled with repeated blows. The comeback almost always went into the finish of his matches.*

Cruiserweight—*A smaller performer who generally weighs 200 pounds or less. Cruiser-weights usually wrestle at a faster pace with more flying maneuvers than their larger peers.*

Cutting a promo—*The act of doing an interview. Usually, a wrestler's promo addresses a feud against another performer. This phrase also can be used when one performer addresses real-life problems with another during an on-air interview.*

Dark match—*A match taped for television that is held just for the live crowd. WWE has traditionally used dark matches as tryouts for unsigned talent.*

Dirt sheets—*Newsletters that describe the behind-the-scenes happenings in wrestling.*

Doing the job—*Being pinned or forced to submit to end a match. For example, Paul "Triple H" Levesque did the job for Dave Batista in the main event of Wrestlemania XXI.*

Downside guarantee—*A common clause in a WWE contract promising the wrestler a set annual salary. The wrestler can then earn more money through other streams such as merchandise sales, wrestling on WWE's non-televised cards, and appearances on pay-per-view shows.*

Extreme-style wrestling—*Matches involving such props as barbed wire, thumbtacks, staple guns, and the like.*

Feeding—*The heel's reaction to the babyface as the babyface makes a comeback. This results in selling the comeback and building the anticipation toward the match finish.*

Finisher—*A wrestler's finishing maneuver, such as Randy Orton's RKO or Chris Benoit's Crippler Crossface.*

Gimmick—*1) A wrestler's in-ring character. Example: Mark Callaway was known as "Mean Mark" before adopting The Undertaker gimmick. 2) Slang for a foreign object like a chain or brass knuckles used in a match.*

Go home—*The concluding of a match. The referee sometimes will tell a wrestler to go home during a televised match if the show is running long.*

Hangman—*A maneuver where the wrestler catches his head between the top and middle ring ropes.*

Hardway juice—*Blood that is drawn without the use of a razorblade. The most common way is when a wrestler takes a legitimate bare-knuckled punch just above the eyebrow, which is an area susceptible to bleeding.*

Heat—*What is generated when a crowd is incited by a wrestler. The term* cheap heat *refers to shortcuts taken by a heel to create a response, like swearing or insulting the town where the show is being held.*

Heel—*A bad guy wrestler whose character should get booed by the crowd.*

High spot—*A move that carries more weight than most and is usually dynamic, such as Chris Jericho's Lionsault or Rob Van Dam's Rolling Thunder. Although such maneuvers should be used sparingly, some novice wrestlers attempt to string a series of high spots into one match to make amends for a lack of ring psychology. The term* high spot *was first used for a series of moves out of a hold leading to a big bump or bumps and appropriate crowd response, followed by the two wrestlers settling back into that same hold. Today, the current generation may call one single move a high spot.*

Hot tag—*At any point in a tag-team match where a beaten-down babyface is finally able to tag his fresh partner. The hot tag often leads into a match finish.*

House show—*A non-televised live wrestling event.*

Jobber—*A performer who regularly loses on television and doesn't receive much if any push. A comparable term for such a performer is* jabroni, *which is a favorite catch phrase of Dwayne "The Rock" Johnson. To soften the blow of such labels, some wrestling promotions refer to jobbers as* enhancement talent. Carpenter *was the phrase used by earlier generations.*

Kay fabe—*The protection of wrestling secrets by its performers. One pro wrestler will tell another to kay fabe when an outsider is in position to hear their conversation.*

Light and loose—*Indicates when a performer is able to perform crisp-looking holds on his opponent without hurting him.*

Making the save—*When a wrestler comes to the aid of another who is being double-teamed (or worse). This phrase also applies when one member of a tag-team interferes to keep his partner from getting pinned.*

Mark—*A wrestling fan who isn't smart to the wrestling business and generally believes at least some of the matches and action isn't predetermined. It is a term taken from the carnies.*

No-show—*A performer who fails to arrive for his scheduled booking.*

Pop—*A large reaction from the crowd. Example: "Stone Cold" Steve Austin would always receive a huge pop when drinking beer inside the ring.*

Program—*A feud between two opponents.*

Putting someone over—*A wrestler who makes the opponent look good through his selling. This phrase also is used when one wrestler is told he is going to lose to another.*

Rib—*A practical joke played by one performer on another.*

Ring psychology—*The art of knowing how to elicit a strong fan response by having the ability to call a match in the ring and adjust according to how the crowd reacts.*

Ring wind—*The conditioning that is built by actually wrestling in a match or stepping inside the ring.*

Road agent—*Someone who works behind the scenes for a promotion and helps run a show by offering suggestions, working with talent, or making sure an event runs smoothly. Ricky Steamboat became a WWE road agent in late 2004.*

Run-in—*When a wrestler, manager, or valet interferes during a match. A run-in often leads to a disqualification finish and is usually done by the heels to gain an advantage over the babyface.*

Screw-job finish—*When a match doesn't have a clear-cut conclusion. Examples include disqualifications, count-outs, or whenever a wrestler cheats and/or needs outside interference to defeat his opponent.*

Selling—*What an opponent does when on the receiving end of a maneuver. For example, any opponent caught in Kurt Angle's ankle lock should sell the move by screaming while hooked and limping afterward.*

Shooter—*A wrestler with the skill to apply holds that can legitimately hurt an opponent. Many of those moves come from the genres of mixed martial arts fighting and amateur wrestling. Ken Shamrock was regarded as one of pro wrestling's top shooters in the late 1990s because of his success in the Ultimate Fighting Championships.*

Showing fire—*Making a comeback seem a legitimate part of the match.*

Slip on a banana peel—*A tactic where the heel makes a mistake and the momentum in the bout shifts from the heel to the babyface. This is the beginning of the babyface's comeback.*

Smark—*Wrestling fans who have varying degrees of knowledge about the inner workings of the wrestling business without ever having been employed in it. Also called* smart mark.

Spot—*A predetermined move during a match.*

Squash—*A lopsided match where one opponent dominates the other.*

Stiff—*When a performer works too heavy handed with his opponent. The phrase* getting stiffed *can refer to a wrestler getting injured through his opponent's carelessness.*

Stretching—*When one performer legitimately dominates another through the use of wrestling or submission holds. Most stretching incidents occur when a wrestler doesn't cooperate with his opponent.*

Turn—*When a wrestler shifts from being a babyface to heel or vice-versa. One of the most memorable heel turns in wrestling history came when perennial babyface Hulk Hogan joined the New World Order in 1996. WWE had a legendary double turn in 1997 when Bret Hart faced Steve Austin at Wrestlemania XIII. Hart entered as a babyface but turned heel shortly thereafter when the crowd had such a strong babyface reaction toward Austin during the match.*

Turnbuckle—*A turnbuckle is metal of varying sizes with hooks on each end and is threaded in the middle. Covered with padding, it is used to tighten the ring ropes and hold them. There are three buckles to each corner. They connect to the ring post through an eyebolt and an O-ring on the rope.*

Tweener—*A performer who works as both a babyface and heel. There are few tweeners in today's generation of wrestlers.*

Work rate—*The standard used to measure how a wrestler performs in the ring. The higher the work rate, the better the wrestler.*